An UNOFFICIAL COOKBOOK for FANS of WILLY WONKA

An UNOFFICIAL COOKBOOK for FANS of WILLY WONKA

Mouthwatering Chocolates, Desserts, and Candy Creations

DAHLIA CLEARWATER

SKYHORSE PUBLISHING

Skyhorse Publishing books may be purchased in bulk at special discounts for sales promotion, corporate gifts, fund-raising, or educational purposes. Special editions can also be created to specifications. For details, contact the Special Sales Department, Skyhorse Publishing, 307 West 36th Street, 11th Floor, New York, NY 10018 or info@skyhorsepublishing.com.

Skyhorse® and Skyhorse Publishing® are registered trademarks of Skyhorse Publishing®, Inc., a Delaware corporation.

Visit our website at www.skyhorsepublishing.com.

10 9 8 7 6 5 4 3 2

Library of Congress Cataloging-in-Publication Data is available on file.

Cover and interior design by Melissa Gerber
Photos used by permission of Shutterstock.com

Print ISBN: 978-1-5107-7475-9
Ebook ISBN: 978-1-5107-7777-4

Printed in United States of America

CONTENTS

WELCOME, MY FRIENDS!

"In your wildest dreams, you could not imagine the marvelous surprises that await you!"

—Willy Wonka, in *Willy Wonka & the Chocolate Factory*

GREETINGS TO YOU, THE LUCKY FINDER OF THIS COOKBOOK!

You're about to enter a world of pure imagination—decadent chocolates, colorful candies, mouthwatering desserts, and fizzy drinks all inspired by one of the greatest movies of all time: *Willy Wonka & the Chocolate Factory*. The 1971 classic has captured hearts and minds for more than fifty years, encouraging viewers to follow their dreams . . . and their taste buds.

Now you can bring Mr. Wonka's greatest creations to life with more than seventy-five treats practically plucked from the film. Enjoy a juicy blueberry pie without any unsettling side effects, savor a Scrumdiddlyumptious Bar (instead of scarfing it like Charlie), and create a gobstopping rainbow cake that would make Slugworth salivate. Every fun and scrumptious recipe is satisfying and delicious!

This is no ordinary cookbook—every recipe inside is Wonka worthy. But there are no nasty tricks, dangerous creations, or eggdicators to judge you. Anything you want to do, do it. If you want to keep things simple, go for it. If you want to decorate a dessert to within an inch of its life, go big. It's your turn to be the Candy Man. Take the keys to this chocolate factory and turn your realities into dreams!

CRUNCHY and SCRUMPTIOUS

TERRIBLY SUSPENSEFUL CANDIED POPCORN

Like Wonka himself, you need something to munch on while you watch wicked children get their just desserts. This white-chocolate-coated popcorn is just the golden ticket. The recipe gives you three different colors of popcorn, but you can make as many varieties as you have bowls and coloring.

MAKES 25 SERVINGS

1⅓ cups popcorn kernels, popped (about 25 cups popped popcorn)

2 cups sugar

½ cup water

1 tablespoon unsalted butter

½ teaspoon each blue, red, and yellow food coloring

¼ teaspoon salt, divided

1. Line 2 large baking sheets with wax paper. Separate popcorn into at least 3 very large bowls.

2. Add sugar, water, and butter to a medium pot over medium-high heat and bring to a boil. Reduce heat to medium and continue to boil, stirring constantly, for 3 minutes.

3. Separate mixture into 3 small bowls. Stir 1 color of food coloring and one-third of salt into each bowl.

4. Working quickly and with 1 bowl at a time, pour colored mixture over popcorn and stir to coat. Spread coated popcorn onto prepared baking sheets and let dry for 1 to 2 hours, until no longer sticky. Mix popcorn together.

5. Store popcorn in an airtight container at room temperature for up to 2 weeks.

SWEETHEART COOKIES

Bedridden or not, you have to give Charlie's grandparents credit for sticking together for so many years! These sweetheart cookies are an adorable way to celebrate their lifelong love. Use the Royal Icing recipe on page 8, dyed red and pink (or any color that tickles your particular fancy), to decorate them.

MAKES 24 COOKIES

2¼ cups all-purpose flour
½ teaspoon baking powder
¼ teaspoon salt
¾ cup unsalted butter,
at room temperature

¾ cup sugar
1 large egg, at room temperature
2 teaspoons pure vanilla extract
¼–½ teaspoon almond extract
Royal Icing (page 8)

1. In a medium bowl, whisk together flour, baking powder, and salt.

2. In a large bowl, add butter and sugar and cream together using an electric mixer fitted with a paddle attachment on high speed. Beat in egg, vanilla, and almond extract on high speed until combined, about 1 minute, scraping down sides and bottom of bowl as needed.

3. Add dry ingredients to wet ingredients and mix on low until combined. If dough is too sticky, mix in 1 more tablespoon of flour.

4. Lightly flour a large piece of parchment or silicone baking mat. Divide dough into 2 equal parts. Use a lightly floured rolling pin to roll out each half of dough until both are ¼ inch thick.

5. Lightly dust 1 flat of dough with flour and cover with parchment. Place remaining flat of dough on top. Cover with plastic wrap or aluminum foil, then refrigerate dough for at least 2 hours and up to 2 days.

6. Once dough is chilled, preheat oven to 350°F. Line 2 large baking sheets with parchment paper or silicone baking mats.

7. Carefully remove top layer of dough from refrigerator. Using a heart-shaped cookie cutter, cut dough into shapes, rerolling scraps as needed. Repeat with remaining layer of dough.

8. Place cookies 3 inches apart on baking sheets. Bake for 11 to 12 minutes or until lightly browned around the edges. Allow cookies to cool on baking sheets for 5 minutes before transferring to a rack to cool completely. When cooled completely, use royal icing to decorate cookies as desired.

Dream Big!

Nothing says you have to stop at icing. While it's still wet, use it as "glue" to tack all kinds of candies onto the sweetheart cookies.

ROYAL ICING

This sweet icing can be used to decorate almost any dessert, but it's especially wonderful for decorating cookies. When properly mixed, the icing should drizzle from the whisk and smooth itself out in the bowl.

MAKES 3 CUPS

4 cups confectioners' sugar, sifted

3 tablespoons meringue powder

9–10 tablespoons room-temperature water

Gel food coloring (optional)

1. Add sugar, meringue powder, and 9 tablespoons of water to a large bowl. Using an electric mixer fitted with a whisk attachment, mix everything together on high speed for 1 to 2 minutes. If finished icing is too thick, mix in more water 1 tablespoon at a time. If too thin, add more confectioners' sugar.

2. To make multiple colors, separate icing into smaller bowls and mix a different color into each bowl.

3. Spoon icing into piping bag (or bags) fitted with piping tip. Decorate your confections. At room temperature, icing should be dry in 2 hours.

CAYENNE CRINKLES *with a* KICK

Sure, you could follow in Wonka's footsteps and stir the odd clothing accessory into your mixtures. But using cayenne pepper instead of soccer cleats results in just as much kick without the rubbery aftertaste. And that hint of heat balances out the sweetness of the chocolate beautifully.

MAKES 20 COOKIES

3 cups confectioners' sugar
¾ cup unsweetened cocoa powder
1 tablespoon cornstarch
¼ teaspoon salt
½ teaspoon cayenne pepper

1 large egg
2 large egg whites
1 teaspoon pure vanilla extract
1 cup semisweet chocolate chips

1. Preheat oven to 350°F and line 2 baking sheets with parchment paper. In a large bowl, stir together sugar, cocoa powder, cornstarch, salt, and cayenne pepper until combined.

2. Stir in egg, egg whites, and vanilla. Continue stirring until sugar dissolves and batter thickens. Stir in chocolate chips until well combined.

3. Spoon the batter, 1 heaping tablespoon at a time and 2 inches apart, onto prepared baking sheets.

4. Bake 1 sheet at a time for 14 minutes or until cookies have expanded and cracked. Allow cookies to cool on baking sheets.

LITTLE GINGERBREAD MEN

These gingerbread men make perfectly scrumptious factory workers—rather than being completely sweet like other cookies, they're just a little spicy. Unfortunately, they won't clean up your messes for you, so you're on your own if you sneak a taste of any experimental treats. Use the royal icing on page 8 to give them their signature overalls and reproachful looks.

MAKES 24 COOKIES

⅔ cup unsalted butter, at room temperature

¾ cup packed light or dark brown sugar

⅔ cup unsulfured molasses

1 large egg, at room temperature

1 teaspoon pure vanilla extract

3½ cups all-purpose flour

1 teaspoon baking soda

½ teaspoon salt

1 tablespoon ground ginger

1 tablespoon ground cinnamon

½ teaspoon ground allspice

½ teaspoon ground cloves

Royal Icing (page 8, optional)

1. Add butter to a large bowl and use an electric mixer fitted with a paddle attachment to beat on medium speed for 1 minute until smooth. Mix in brown sugar and molasses until combined and creamy, scraping down sides and bottom of bowl as needed. Next, beat in egg and vanilla on high speed for 2 minutes, scraping down bowl as needed.

2. In another large bowl, whisk together flour, baking soda, salt, ginger, cinnamon, allspice, and cloves until combined. Using mixer on low speed, slowly incorporate wet ingredients into dry until combined. Divide dough in half, tightly wrap each half in plastic wrap, and pat down to create a disk shape. Let disks chill overnight.

3. Preheat oven to 350°F. Line 2 large baking sheets with parchment paper or silicone baking mats.

4. Remove 1 disk of chilled dough from refrigerator. Generously flour a work surface, your hands, and a rolling pin. Roll disk out to about ¼ inch thick. Use your fingers to mend any cracks.

5. Use a gingerbread-man cutter to cut dough into shapes, rerolling scraps as needed. Place gingerbread men 1 inch apart on prepared baking sheets. Repeat with remaining disk of dough.

6. Bake cookies for 8 to 10 minutes. Allow cookies to cool for 5 minutes on baking sheet before transferring to a rack to finish cooling. When cooled completely, decorate with royal icing as desired.

Dream Big!

Divide the icing in 3, leaving 1 white and dyeing the other 2 orange and green respectively to fill in the factory workers' other details.

10-GALLON COWBOY COOKIES

Full of chocolate, nuts, oats, and cinnamon, these flavor-packed cookies have everything a cowboy needs to sustain him out on the range. Browned butter takes things up a notch, giving them a star quality. But beware: these cookies are so big and hearty they could crush a miniaturized boy.

MAKES 24 TO 36 COOKIES

1 cup salted butter, at room temperature, divided
1 cup packed brown sugar
½ cup granulated sugar
2 large eggs
2 teaspoons pure vanilla extract
2 cups all-purpose flour

1 teaspoon baking soda
½ teaspoon ground cinnamon
1½ cups old-fashioned rolled oats
1 cup chopped pecans
1 cup coconut flakes
2 cups chocolate chips
Flaky salt (optional)

1. In a medium saucepan, melt and brown ½ cup of the butter over medium heat, letting it cook for 3 to 5 minutes or until foamy and golden brown. Pour butter into a large, heatproof mixing bowl and stir to cool. Let cool to room temperature, about 30 minutes.

2. Preheat oven to 350°F. Line 2 large baking sheets with parchment paper.

3. Add remaining ½ cup butter, brown sugar, and granulated sugar to the mixing bowl with browned butter. Combine using an electric mixer on medium-high speed for 2 to 3 minutes or until lightened.

4. Reduce mixer to low and beat in eggs and vanilla until smooth, scraping down sides and bottom of bowl as needed.

5. In a medium bowl, whisk together flour, baking soda, and cinnamon. Add to butter mixture in thirds, mixing each on low speed until fully incorporated and scraping down sides and bottom of bowl as needed. Mix in oats, pecans, coconut flakes, and chocolate chips on low speed until combined.

6. Using a 2-tablespoon cookie scoop, drop cookie dough onto prepared baking sheets 2 inches apart. Bake for 12 to 14 minutes, until golden brown. Let cookies cool for 2 minutes on baking sheets before transferring to a rack to cool completely. Finish with a sprinkle of flaky salt, if desired.

TIE-DYED DOUGHNUT HOLES

With some creative decorating, these delicious fried doughnut holes transform into a candy-like treat. They might be light as air, but you'll be better off eating them than kicking them around. Just make sure you have a deep-fry thermometer handy and use the stove to warm up the oil instead of any nearby coats.

MAKES 24 DOUGHNUT HOLES

For the Glaze

2 cups confectioners' sugar, sifted

1 teaspoon lemon extract

2 tablespoons whole milk

Gel food coloring, rainbow colors

For the Doughnut Holes

5 cups vegetable oil

1 cup milk

1 large egg

2 cups all-purpose flour

2 tablespoons granulated sugar

4½ teaspoons baking powder

½ teaspoon salt

4 tablespoons unsalted butter, melted

1. To make glaze: Add confectioners' sugar to a large bowl, then whisk in lemon extract and milk. If glaze is too thin, add confectioners' sugar. If too thick, add milk 1 teaspoon at a time.

2. Pour half of glaze into a shallow bowl or rimmed plate. Add 1 or 2 drops of each food coloring and use a toothpick to swirl them together until marbled.

3. To make doughnuts: Add 2 inches of vegetable oil to a large, heavy-bottomed pot over medium-high heat and bring to 350°F on deep-fry thermometer. Line a baking sheet with paper towels.

4. In a small bowl, whisk together milk and egg.

5. In a medium bowl, whisk together flour, granulated sugar, baking powder, and salt. Stir wet mixture into dry mixture, then stir in melted butter until a soft dough forms.

6. Drop dough by the tablespoon into oil, being careful not to crowd the pan. Fry doughnuts, flipping frequently, for about 2 minutes until evenly golden brown. Use a slotted spoon to transfer doughnuts to prepared baking sheet.

7. Allow doughnuts to cool slightly before moving them to a plate. Place a cooling rack on baking sheet. One at a time, dip doughnuts into glaze and transfer to rack to allow excess to drain. When colors start to fade, pour remaining glaze into glaze bowl and swirl in more food coloring. Dip remaining doughnuts in glaze, continuing to transfer them to rack. Serve warm.

BREAKFAST for DESSERT CEREAL BARS

You might not be able to enjoy a three-course meal in one bite, but you can make a crunchy, gooey, three-ingredient, breakfast-inspired dessert bar that tastes just as amazing. And the only side effect of this treat is joy. Not a fan of fruity cereals? Swap in a classic, like chocolate rice cereal.

MAKES 18 BARS

Nonstick cooking spray

3 tablespoons unsalted butter

10 ounces marshmallows

6 cups colorful fruit-flavored cereal

1. Spray a 13 × 9-inch baking dish with nonstick cooking spray.

2. Melt butter in a medium pan over medium low heat.

3. Stir in marshmallows until fully melted.

4. Remove mixture from heat and stir in cereal until well combined.

5. Coat a spatula with nonstick cooking spray and use it to firmly pack cereal mixture into prepared baking dish.

6. Let mixture cool completely at room temperature before cutting into 18 bars.

SQUARE DEAL BROWNIE BARS

Sam would love these oh-so-American nut-filled brownies, which are as chocolatey a treat as any at the factory. Thankfully, they're also simpler and more straightforward to whip up than a car contract. You can use whichever kind of nut you like, but almonds give these brownies candy-bar vibes.

MAKES 16 BROWNIES

1 cup salted butter, melted
3 large eggs, at room temperature
2 teaspoons pure vanilla extract
½ teaspoon sea salt
¾ cup granulated sugar
1 cup packed light brown sugar

¾ cup unsweetened cocoa powder
1 cup all-purpose flour
4 ounces bittersweet chocolate chips
¾ cup chopped nuts

1. Preheat oven to 350°F. Grease a 9-inch square baking pan and line with parchment paper, leaving "wings" for easy removal.

2. In a large bowl, whisk together melted butter, eggs, vanilla, and salt until well combined. Stir in granulated sugar and brown sugar, mixing well.

3. Sift cocoa powder and flour into bowl and use a spatula to fold in until well combined.

4. Fold in chocolate chips and nuts.

5. Add batter to prepared pan and smooth to the edges.

6. Bake for 25 to 30 minutes, until center is just set.

7. Cool brownies in pan for 20 minutes before transferring to a wire rack to cool completely.

BUZZ-WORTHY HONEY NUT BARS

Wonka would probably be better off putting his honeybees' hard work toward something that doesn't blow up children, like these incredible bars. The honey in these nutty treats creates the perfect balance of salty and sweet, and enjoying them won't require any life-saving intervention.

MAKES 9 BARS

For the Shortbread Base
½ cup unsalted butter,
at room temperature
½ cup confectioners' sugar
1 cup all-purpose or cake flour

For the Filling
6 tablespoons unsalted butter

½ cup packed light brown sugar
½ cup honey
1 cup walnuts, coarsely chopped
¼ cup whipping cream
Pinch of salt
1 teaspoon pure vanilla extract
½ teaspoon lemon zest

1. Preheat oven to 350°F. Grease an 8-inch square baking pan and line with parchment paper, leaving "wings" for easy removal.

2. To make shortbread base: Add butter and confectioners' sugar to a large bowl and mix until creamy. Use a spatula to stir in flour and create a soft dough.

3. Press dough evenly into bottom of prepared baking dish.

4. Prick dough all over with a fork and blind bake for 15 to 20 minutes, until just beginning to brown at edges. Transfer to a wire rack while preparing filling.

5. To make filling: Add butter, brown sugar, and honey to a medium saucepan and bring to a boil over medium heat. Continue cooking, stirring occasionally, for 5 minutes.

6. Remove from heat and immediately stir in walnuts, cream, salt, vanilla, and lemon zest.

7. Carefully pour mixture evenly over shortbread crust and return dish to oven to bake for 20 minutes. Do not overbake, as filling will harden as it cools.

8. Remove dish from the oven and let stand for 5 to 10 minutes on a wire rack to cool.

9. While still warm, carefully run a smooth-bladed knife around edges. Let cool completely on rack or transfer to refrigerator to cool for 1 hour before cutting into squares.

STRAWBERRY LEMON PIE BARS

When "The Candy Man" randomly pops into your head, that's the universe's way of telling you to make the song's signature dessert: strawberry lemon pie. This sweet, tart, and crumbly take on the pie really does taste like a rainbow soaked in the sun! You can use frozen berries, but you'll need to thaw and drain them, add 2 tablespoons flour to their mixture, and add up to 15 minutes to the baking time.

MAKES 9 BARS

For the Crumb Crust
½ cup unsalted butter, melted
½ cup granulated sugar
¼ cup packed light brown sugar
1½ cups all-purpose flour
Pinch of salt

For the Filling
1 large egg
½ cup plain or vanilla Greek yogurt
⅓ cup granulated sugar
2 tablespoons lemon juice
2 teaspoons pure vanilla extract
¼ cup all-purpose flour

For the Fruit Layer
2 heaping cups diced fresh strawberries
⅓ cup granulated sugar
2 tablespoons lemon juice
2 teaspoons lemon zest
2 teaspoons cornstarch

1. Preheat oven to 350°F. Line an 8-inch square pan with nonstick aluminum foil and grease foil.

2. To make crumb crust: In a large bowl, whisk together melted butter and sugars. Stir in flour and salt.

3. Set ¾ cup of crumbly mixture aside. Pack remaining mixture evenly into bottom of prepared pan to create crust.

4. To make filling: In another large bowl with an electric mixer, beat together egg, yogurt, granulated sugar, lemon juice, and vanilla. Add flour and mix until well combined and smooth.

5. Pour filling evenly over crust and use a spatula to smooth it out.

6. To make fruit layer: Add all ingredients to a large bowl and stir to combine. Use a spatula to evenly top filling with fruit mixture.

7. Sprinkle reserved crumb mixture evenly over fruit and bake for about 60 minutes until fruit layer begins actively bubbling and crumble topping is beginning to brown.

8. Transfer pan to a wire rack to cool for at least 2 hours, then transfer to refrigerator for 2 more hours. When cold, slice and serve.

DECADENT and DELECTABLE

COLORFUL CHAOS RAINBOW BARK

As colorful and chaotic as Wonka himself, this white-chocolate bark it not just a delightful treat on its own—it's also the ideal topper to decorate almost any dessert. It's deceptively simple with just two ingredients. Break it up and use it to add flare to your fudges, cakes, and milkshakes.

MAKES 12 SERVINGS

1 (12-oz) bag white chocolate chips

2 tablespoons colorful sprinkles

1. Line a baking sheet with wax paper.

2. Add chocolate to a large, microwave-safe bowl and microwave in 30-second increments, stirring after each, until melted.

3. Pour melted chocolate onto prepared baking sheet. While still warm, scatter rainbow sprinkles all over.

4. Transfer baking sheet to refrigerator until bark hardens. Use your hands or a heavy kitchen tool to break bark into uneven pieces.

Dream Big!

Add even more colorful chaos by using a toothpick to swirl multiple colors of gel food coloring through the bark and topping it off with even more candy.

CHOCOLATE-RASPBERRY GOURDS

Veruca's greedy nature means no one thinks twice when she scoops messy handfuls of chocolate out of multicolored gourds in the Chocolate Room. But putting that delicious filling into poppable chocolate-raspberry truffles offers you the same gorge-worthy flavor with a more dignified experience.

MAKES 30 TRUFFLES

1 (10-oz) package frozen raspberries, thawed

¼ cup confectioners' sugar

1 pound semisweet or bittersweet chocolate, finely chopped

¾ cup heavy whipping cream

2 tablespoons light corn syrup

1 pound semisweet baking chocolate, finely chopped

1. Add raspberries to a blender or food processor and blend until liquid.

2. Strain raspberry puree over a small saucepan to remove seeds. Stir in confectioners' sugar and cook mixture over medium heat, stirring frequently, until thickened and reduced by about half. Set aside.

3. Add semisweet or bittersweet chocolate to a large bowl. Add cream to a small saucepan and cook over medium heat until it just begins to simmer at edges. Then pour hot cream over chopped chocolate and let sit for 1 to 2 minutes.

4. When chocolate is softened, whisk in cream until well combined and smooth. Then whisk in corn syrup and raspberry puree to finish ganache.

5. Cover ganache with plastic wrap, pressing it against chocolate's surface, and refrigerate until set, at least 2 hours.

6. Line a baking sheet with wax paper. Using a small candy scoop or teaspoon, scoop ganache and roll into small balls, placing them 2 inches apart on prepared baking sheet. Transfer baking sheet to freezer to chill for 2 hours or until firm.

7. Add baking chocolate to a large, microwave-safe bowl. Microwave in 30-second increments, stirring after each, until melted and smooth. Allow coating to cool until just warm.

8. Working quickly, use a fork to dip each truffle into melted chocolate, allow excess to drain, then place dipped truffle back on baking sheet. If truffles begin to soften, refreeze them before continuing to dip them.

9. Transfer finished truffles to refrigerator and let chocolate set for about 30 minutes. Store in an airtight container in the refrigerator for up to 1 week.

Dream Big!

Create more colorful gourds by melting white chocolate chips instead of baker's chocolate, separating it into smaller bowls, and mixing 1 or 2 drops of gel food coloring into each. Then top each truffle with rainbow sprinkles.

QUICKER LIQUOR-INFUSED CANDIES

As American poet Ogden Nash said and Mr. Wonka repeated, "Candy is dandy, but liquor is quicker." These boozy treats are so divine that they'll leave you with a golden twinkle in your eye. But they're just as twinkly with 2 teaspoons of pure vanilla flavoring in place of the liqueur if you prefer your chocolate alcohol free.

MAKES 40 CANDIES

Unsalted butter

2 cups sugar

½ cup water

¼ cup half-and-half or light cream

1 tablespoon light corn syrup

2 tablespoons amaretto or coffee liqueur

1 pound semisweet baking chocolate, finely chopped

1. Line a baking sheet with wax paper. Butter sides of a heavy 2-quart saucepan.

2. Combine sugar, water, half-and-half, and light corn syrup in prepared saucepan. Bring mixture to a boil over medium-high heat, stirring constantly, until sugar dissolves, 5 to 6 minutes. Avoid splashing mixture on sides of pan.

3. Reduce heat to medium-low and insert a candy thermometer into the mixture. Continue cooking, stirring occasionally, until temperature reaches 240°F, 15 to 20 minutes.

4. Remove saucepan from heat. Let mixture cool, undisturbed, to 110°F, about 45 minutes. Remove candy thermometer from saucepan. Stir in liqueur until mixture is creamy and slightly firm, about 10 minutes.

5. Drop candies by the tablespoon onto prepared baking sheet and roll them into balls. Let stand at room temperature until dry, about 20 minutes.

6. Add baking chocolate to a large, microwave-safe bowl and microwave in 30-second increments, stirring after each, until melted and smooth. Use a fork to dip each candy into melted chocolate, allow excess to drain, then place dipped truffle back on baking sheet. Store in an airtight container in a cool, dry place for up to 1 week.

LIGHTNING in a CHOCOLATE BAR

The news anchor who describes the golden tickets as "five lucky bolts of lightning ready to strike without notice" isn't wrong, especially when you think of the fate of most recipients. This honeycomb candy brings the crackle of lightning without any scary repercussions and tastes as sweet as finding the prize. For the crunchiest bars, enjoy these the day you make them.

MAKES 26 BARS

Nonstick cooking spray

For the Honeycomb Candy

2 cups sugar

½ cup light corn syrup

¼ cup honey

¼ cup water

1 heaping tablespoon baking soda

For the Chocolate Coating

12 ounces dark chocolate, roughly chopped

2 tablespoons shortening

1. Line a 13 × 9-inch baking pan with nonstick aluminum foil, leaving "wings" for easy removal, and grease the foil with nonstick cooking spray.

2. To make honeycomb candy: In a large saucepan over medium heat, combine sugar, corn syrup, honey, and water and stir until sugar is completely incorporated. Remove stray sugar crystals by wiping the sides of the pan with a wet pastry brush.

3. Insert a candy thermometer into mixture and let it continue to cook, without stirring, until candy reaches 300°F.

4. Remove pan from heat and add baking soda, quickly and carefully whisking it into candy until fully incorporated. Mixture will foam and expand.

5. Carefully pour hot candy into prepared baking pan. Allow it to cool and harden completely, then use aluminum foil to lift candy out of pan.

6. Use a serrated knife to score candy into 13 strips, about 1 inch wide each. Then score across the center of the strips to create 26 small bars. Break candy along score lines.

7. To make chocolate coating: Combine chocolate and shortening in a large, microwave-safe bowl. Microwave in 30-second increments, stirring after each, until chocolate is completely melted.

8. Line a baking sheet with wax paper. Drop a honeycomb bar in chocolate, using forks or a slotted spoon to ensure it's completely coated, then place on prepared baking sheet.

9. Repeat with remaining honeycomb and refrigerate until chocolate is set. Allow bars to come to room temperature before serving.

FABULOUS ROCKY ROAD FUDGE

When Augustus says he plans on costing Mr. Wonka a fortune in fudge, he probably never imagines that he'll be suctioned into the Fudge Room and ruin the batch. Like most of the ticket winners, he'd have been better off making his own at home. This recipe adds nuts and marshmallows for a fudge you won't be able to get enough of either.

MAKES 48 PIECES

1½ teaspoons plus 1 tablespoon unsalted butter, divided

2 cups semisweet chocolate chips

1 (14-oz) can sweetened condensed milk

2 cups salted peanuts

1 (10-oz) package miniature marshmallows

1. Line a 13 × 9-inch baking pan with nonstick aluminum foil, leaving "wings" for easy removal. Grease foil with 1½ teaspoons of the butter.

2. Add chocolate chips, sweetened condensed milk, and remaining 1 tablespoon butter to a large saucepan over medium heat. Cook and stir until mixture is combined and smooth.

3. Remove from heat and stir in peanuts. Allow mixture to cool for 5 minutes before folding in marshmallows.

4. Immediately spread mixture into prepared pan. Refrigerate until set, at least 4 hours.

5. Lift fudge out of pan using foil wings and cut into small squares.

Dream Big!

Use multicolored marshmallows (like the ones on page 90, chopped up) instead of plain white ones. You can also top the fudge with sprinkles and candy before it sets.

SCRUMDIDDLYUMPTIOUS BARS

Anyone can understand Charlie's desire to devour his unexpected treat whole, but you'll want to savor these no-bake bars. With creamy peanuty butter, sweet butterscotch, and milk chocolate, they're called Scrumdiddlyumptious for a reason!

MAKES 36 TO 48 BARS

8 ounces buttery crackers, divided
1 cup unsalted butter, cubed
½ cup whole milk
2 cups graham cracker crumbs
1 cup packed light brown sugar

⅓ cup granulated sugar
⅔ cup creamy peanut butter
½ cup milk chocolate chips
½ cup butterscotch chips

1. Cover bottom of an ungreased 13 × 9-inch baking pan with one-third of crackers.

2. Melt butter in a small saucepan over medium-high heat. Add milk, graham cracker crumbs, and brown sugar and granulated sugar and bring mixture to a boil. Continue cooking and stirring for 5 more minutes.

3. Pour half of mixture evenly over crackers. Layer half of remaining crackers on top followed by remaining sugar mixture. Top with remaining crackers.

4. In a small saucepan over low heat, combine peanut butter, chocolate chips, and butterscotch chips until melted and smooth. Spread mixture over crackers. Transfer pan to refrigerator and chill until set, about 1 hour. Cut into small squares, serve, and savor.

FUDGE MALLOW COOKIES

This marshmallowy birthday treat may not earn Charlie his golden ticket, but you'll feel like a winner when you taste it. Fudge Mallows fly off the candy-store shelves for a reason. You can use graham crackers instead of whole-wheat crackers if you prefer, but it makes for a crumblier cookie.

MAKES 6 COOKIES

6 round whole-wheat crackers

6 tablespoons marshmallow creme

4 ounces bittersweet chocolate

2 teaspoons vegetable oil

1. Line a baking sheet with parchment paper or a silicone baking mat.

2. Place crackers on prepared baking sheet 2 inches apart and top each with 1 tablespoon of marshmallow creme.

3. Transfer baking sheet to freezer until creme is set, 15 to 20 minutes.

4. When creme is chilled, add chocolate and oil to a small, microwave-safe bowl and microwave in 30-second increments, stirring after each, until chocolate is melted and smooth.

5. Using a slotted spoon, hold 1 cookie over bowl and spoon melted chocolate over it, allowing excess to drain, until cookie is completely coated. Return finished cookie to baking sheet and repeat with remaining cookies.

6. Transfer baking sheet back to freezer until chocolate is set, at least 30 minutes.

7. Serve immediately or store cookies in an airtight container in refrigerator.

CAKE POPS *for the* PICKING

If colorful bits of cake really grew on trees, there'd be orchards of the sweets on every corner. Until that dreamy day, you can whip up these delicious dipped cake pops any time you like. You'll mix these with love (i.e., make them from scratch), but you can substitute boxed cake mix and packaged frosting if you're in a hurry. You just need lollipop sticks and a block of Styrofoam.

MAKES 40 CAKE POPS

Nonstick cooking spray

1⅔ cups all-purpose flour

½ teaspoon baking powder

¼ teaspoon baking soda

½ teaspoon salt

½ cup unsalted butter, at room temperature

1 cup sugar

1 large egg, at room temperature

2 teaspoons pure vanilla extract

1 cup whole milk or buttermilk

1 cup sprinkles, divided

1 cup Vanilla Buttercream Frosting (page 35)

2 pounds white candy melts or white chocolate

1. Preheat to 350°F. Coat a 9-inch springform pan or an 11 × 7-inch pan with nonstick cooking spray.

2. In a large bowl, whisk together flour, baking powder, baking soda, and salt.

3. In another large bowl with an electric mixer fitted with a paddle, cream butter and sugar, about 2 minutes. Add egg and vanilla and beat on high speed until combined, scraping down sides and bottom of bowl as needed.

4. Add dry ingredients and milk to wet ingredients and mix on low speed until combined, then whisk by hand to break up any lumps. Pour batter evenly into prepared pan.

5. Bake for 30 to 36 minutes or until cake reaches an internal temperature of 200°F to 210°F. Transfer pan to a wire rack to cool completely (overnight is best).

6. Line a baking sheet with wax paper or a silicone baking mat. Crumble cooled cake into a large bowl and fold in ½ cup of the sprinkles. Add frosting and use an electric mixer on low speed to mix until well combined.

7. Measure out 1 tablespoon of cake mixture and roll into a ball. Place ball on prepared baking sheet and repeat with remaining cake mixture. Transfer baking sheet to refrigerator and let chill for 2 hours.

(continued on page 34)

(continued from page 32)

8. When cake balls are chilled, place white candies in large, microwave-safe bowl or measuring cup and microwave in 30-second increments, stirring after each, until melted and smooth. Pour remaining sprinkles into a small bowl.

9. Working with 2 or 3 cake balls at a time and leaving remaining balls in refrigerator, dip a lollipop stick about ½ inch into coating, then insert into center of cake ball, stopping halfway through. Coat cake ball completely. Allow excess coating to drip off, then dip cake pop into sprinkles and place upright in a Styrofoam block. Repeat with remaining cake balls.

10. Allow coating to set for 1 hour before serving or store pops in refrigerator for up to 1 week.

Dream Big!

Create a bouquet of pastel-colored cake pops by dividing the melted white candies or chocolate into several smaller bowls and stirring in gel food coloring to dye each a different color before dipping.

VANILLA *or* CHOCOLATE BUTTERCREAM FROSTING

You can't go wrong with a classic vanilla buttercream frosting. It's as adaptable as a worker who has to stop what they're doing every few minutes to save naughty children from themselves. Add a bit of gel food coloring and/or sprinkles to decorate this yummy frosting. It can top off almost any recipe, including cupcakes, cakes, fudges, and even milkshakes and hot chocolates.

MAKES 2½ CUPS

1 cup unsalted butter,
at room temperature

4½–5 cups confectioners' sugar

¼ cup heavy cream,
at room temperature

2 teaspoons pure vanilla extract

⅛ teaspoon salt

1. Add butter to a large bowl and use an electric mixer fitted with a paddle attachment to beat on medium speed until creamy, about 2 minutes. Add 4½ cups of the confectioners' sugar, heavy cream, vanilla, and salt and mix on low speed for 30 seconds. Increase to medium-high speed and continue mixing for 2 minutes. Be careful not to overmix.

2. If frosting is thin, mix in remaining ½ cup confectioners' sugar, 1 tablespoon at a time, until desired consistency is reached. Store in an airtight container in refrigerator for up to 1 week or in freezer for up to 3 months.

note: To make chocolate buttercream frosting, use 3½ to 4 cups confectioners' sugar and ¾ cup unsweetened cocoa powder.

DECEPTIVELY DELICIOUS CAKESICLES

If Wonka teaches his tour-takers anything, it's to expect the unexpected. Looking at these colorful pops, you might never expect that they're made with rich, chocolatey brownies and not ice cream. But their secret identity makes them all the more delicious. Just make sure you have cakesicle molds and sticks handy.

MAKES 8 CAKESICLES

Nonstick cooking spray

½ cup plus 2 tablespoons unsalted butter, at room temperature

1 cup sugar

2 large eggs, at room temperature

1½ teaspoons pure vanilla extract

7 ounces semisweet chocolate chips

⅔ cup all-purpose flour

½ teaspoon salt

1 tablespoon unsweetened cocoa powder

¼ cup Chocolate Buttercream Frosting (page 35)

2 cups white chocolate chips

Gel food coloring

1. Preheat oven to 350°F. Line a 9-inch square pan with parchment paper and spray the paper lightly with nonstick cooking spray.

2. In a large bowl with an electric mixer fitted with a paddle attachment, cream butter and sugar. Add eggs and vanilla and beat on high speed until combined, 2 to 3 minutes, scraping down sides and bottom of bowl as needed.

3. Add semisweet chips to a large, microwave-safe bowl and microwave in 30-second increments, stirring after each, until melted and smooth.

4. Add melted chocolate to butter mixture and mix until combined. Add flour, salt, and cocoa powder and mix until well combined.

5. Pour batter into prepared pan and bake for 35 to 40 minutes. Transfer pan to wire rack to cool completely. (Overnight is best.)

6. Crumble brownies into a large bowl. Stir in chocolate frosting until well combined.

7. Add white chocolate chips to a large, microwave-safe bowl and microwave in 30-second increments, stirring after each, until melted and smooth. Stir in gel food coloring 1 drop at a time until desired color is reached.

(continued on page 38)

(continued from page 36)

8. Spread 1 tablespoon of melted white chocolate into each cakesicle mold. Transfer molds to refrigerator to set, 5 to 10 minutes. Cover thin areas with more white chocolate as needed and refrigerate again until set.

9. Remove molds from refrigerator and fill each with 2 tablespoons of brownie mixture, gently pressing it into mold.

10. Spread 1 tablespoon of melted white chocolate over each cakesicle, then transfer molds back to refrigerator to set, 5 to 10 minutes.

11. When chocolate has set, gently remove cakesicles from molds and serve.

Dream Big!

Make multiple colors by dividing the melted white chocolate into several bowls and coloring each separately. Then dip or drizzle finished cakesicles with opposite colors and top them off with sprinkles.

Good Egg
Peanut-Butter Chocolates

As mouthwatering as enormous hunks of solid chocolate sound, this twist on Wonka's golden eggs is even better. The gilded goods are on the inside: a creamy peanut butter filling. And unlike more ... demanding ... candies, these are incredibly easy to make and sure to please.

MAKES 18 CHOCOLATES

6 tablespoons unsalted butter, at room temperature

1 cup creamy peanut butter

2½ cups confectioners' sugar

½ teaspoon pure vanilla extract

⅛ teaspoon salt

12 ounces semisweet chocolate, coarsely chopped

1 teaspoon vegetable oil

Coarse sea salt (optional)

1. Line a large baking sheet with parchment paper or a silicone baking mat.

2. In a large bowl with an electric mixer fitted with a paddle attachment, beat butter on medium-high speed until creamy, about 2 minutes. Add peanut butter and mix until combined, about 1 minute. Add confectioners' sugar, vanilla, and salt, and mix on low for 2 minutes until well combined and crumbly.

3. Measure out 1 ounce of peanut butter mixture and roll it into a ball, then use your hands to create an egg shape roughly ¾ inch thick. Place formed egg on prepared baking sheet and repeat with remaining peanut butter mixture. If mixture is too soft, chill in refrigerator for 15 minutes.

4. Transfer baking sheet to refrigerator and let eggs chill for at least 1 hour and up to 1 day. When eggs have almost finished chilling, add chocolate and oil to a large, microwave-safe bowl and microwave in 30-second increments, stirring after each, until melted and smooth. Let hot chocolate cool for 6 to 8 minutes until just warm.

5. Remove eggs from refrigerator. Working quickly, use a fork to dip each egg into melted chocolate, let excess drain, and place coated egg back on baking sheet. If remaining eggs begin to soften, refrigerate for 5 to 10 minutes before continuing to dip them.

6. Drizzle chocolate-dipped eggs with remaining chocolate and sprinkle with sea salt, if desired. Then transfer baking sheet to refrigerator and let finished chocolates cool until set, at least 30 minutes, before serving. Store separated by wax paper in airtight container in refrigerator for up to 2 weeks.

A Berry Sweet Twist Cake

As Charlie's mom wisely tells him, things change when you least expect it. And this colorful Swiss roll is just as delightful as the twist of fate the Bucket family encounters. This recipe calls for a filling of strawberry jam, but you could use Vanilla Buttercream Frosting (page 35) or Whipped Cream (page 94) instead.

MAKES 12 SERVINGS

Nonstick cooking spray

For the Cake

1 cup all-purpose flour

1 teaspoon baking powder

½ teaspoon salt

4 large eggs, at room temperature

¾ cup granulated sugar

2 tablespoons vegetable oil

2 tablespoons buttermilk

1 teaspoon apple cider vinegar

1 teaspoon pure vanilla extract

⅛ teaspoon pink gel food coloring

1½ cups strawberry jam

For the Glaze

1½ cups confectioners' sugar, plus more for dusting

2–4 tablespoons whole milk

½ teaspoon almond extract

2 tablespoons sprinkles

1. Preheat oven to 350°F. Coat a 15 × 10-inch jelly roll pan with nonstick cooking spray, cover it with parchment paper, and then spray the parchment paper. Spread a tea towel on a flat work surface and dust it with confectioners' sugar.

2. To make cake: In a medium mixing bowl, combine flour, baking powder, and salt.

3. In a large mixing bowl with an electric mixer, beat eggs on high speed for 3 minutes. Continue mixing as you slowly add granulated sugar. Add oil, buttermilk, vinegar, vanilla, and food coloring and mix for 1 minute more.

4. Mix dry ingredients into wet ingredients until just combined, then spread batter evenly into prepared pan. Bake for 12 to 15 minutes or until cake springs back when touched.

5. Immediately invert cake onto prepared towel, remove parchment paper, and then carefully roll cake up in towel from short end to short end. Transfer rolled cake to a wire rack to cool completely.

6. When cool, unroll cake and spread jam evenly over it. Use the towel to roll cake back up, this time without rolling the towel into it, and place it seam-side down on a serving platter. Cover cake with plastic wrap and transfer to refrigerator for at least 1 hour.

7. To make glaze: When cake is chilled, in a medium bowl, combine confectioners' sugar with 2 tablespoons of the milk and almond extract. If glaze is too thick, add milk 1 tablespoon at a time. Pour glaze over cake, top with sprinkles, and serve.

BLUE SKIES AHEAD CUPCAKES

Blasting off from the Chocolate Factory into the blue skies above, Charlie and Grandpa Joe get the sweet surprise of a lifetime. So it's only fitting that these luscious cupcakes contain a decadent surprise of their own. Make sure not to overbake them so they stay moist.

MAKES 18 CUPCAKES

For the Cupcakes

1 cup granulated sugar

1 cup buttermilk

¼ cup canola oil

1 teaspoon pure vanilla extract

1½ cups all-purpose flour

⅓ cup unsweetened cocoa powder

1 teaspoon baking soda

½ teaspoon salt

For the Filling

6 ounces reduced-fat cream cheese

2 tablespoons confectioners' sugar

1 large egg

2 chocolate-covered caramel-nougat candy bars, finely chopped

For the Frosting

1 cup Vanilla Buttercream Frosting (page 35)

Blue gel food coloring (optional)

1. Preheat oven to 350°F. Line 1½ muffin tins with paper or silicone cups.

2. To make cupcakes: In a large bowl with an electric mixer on medium-high speed, beat granulated sugar, buttermilk, oil, and vanilla until well combined. In another bowl, combine flour, cocoa, baking soda, and salt. Gradually beat dry ingredients into wet ingredients until combined.

3. To make filling: In a small bowl, mix cream cheese and confectioners' sugar on low speed until light and fluffy. Mix in egg, scraping down sides and bottom of bowl as needed. Use a spatula to fold in chopped candy bars.

4. Fill each muffin cup one-third full with batter. Drop heaping tablespoons of filling into center of each cup, pressing into batter. Bake for 20 minutes or until a toothpick inserted into cake part of cupcake comes out dry but not clean. Allow cupcakes to cool in pan for 10 minutes before transferring to wire racks to cool completely before frosting.

5. To make frosting: Follow directions on page 35, then mix in 2 or 3 drops food coloring, if desired. Spoon frosting into a piping bag with a star tip, and frost cooled cupcakes.

STRETCHY and SWEET

Not-So-Lifesaving Lollipops

Lollipops may make terrible lifesaving devices when someone falls into a chocolate river, but as far as candies go, they're pretty great. And they're easier to make than you might think. Just save this recipe for a sunny day—high humidity makes for gooey lollipops.

MAKES 8 TO 12 LOLLIPOPS

Nonstick cooking spray
1 cup sugar
½ cup light corn syrup

¼ cup water
1½ teaspoons favorite candy flavoring
2 drops gel food coloring

1. Spray a paper towel with nonstick cooking spray, then wipe lollipop molds to lightly grease them. Place lollipop sticks in molds.

2. Add sugar, corn syrup, and water to a medium saucepan over medium-high heat and stir until sugar dissolves, continuously brushing sugar crystals from sides of pan using a wet pastry brush.

3. Bring mixture to a boil, then insert a candy thermometer into the mixture. Let it cook undisturbed until candy reaches 300°F.

4. Remove saucepan from heat and allow it to sit until simmering stops completely. Stir in flavoring and food coloring.

5. Spoon hot candy into molds, filling each cavity and covering each stick. Let lollipops cool completely, about 10 minutes, before removing from mold.

SNAPPY COMEBACK SALTWATER TAFFY

Veruca doesn't make many smart moves in the movie, but chewing on soft, stretchy taffy instead of snapping back when Violet tells her to "can it" is one of them. With saltwater taffy this flavorful, you'll be happy to take a moment to savor it. Using a candy thermometer will make the process as smooth as the taffy itself.

MAKES 30 PIECES

Nonstick cooking spray
1 cup sugar
1 tablespoon cornstarch
1 tablespoon unsalted butter, at room temperature
⅔ cup light corn syrup

1 teaspoon salt
½ cup water
1 teaspoon pure vanilla extract
½ teaspoon favorite candy flavoring
2 drops gel food coloring

1. Coat a large, heatproof baking dish with nonstick cooking spray.

2. Add sugar to a large pot fitted with a candy thermometer. Sift in cornstarch and whisk until well combined. Add butter, corn syrup, salt, water, vanilla, and candy flavoring and whisk to combine.

3. Turn heat to medium and cook just until mixture reaches 250°F, then remove from heat immediately. Stir in food coloring until well combined.

4. Carefully pour hot candy into prepared dish and let cool until you can comfortably handle it, 5 to 10 minutes.

5. Using your hands, pull mixture out to at least 12 inches long and fold and stretch it repeatedly for 10 to 15 minutes. Taffy should be opaque when finished.

6. When taffy becomes harder to work, drop onto a greased work surface and roll into a log about 30 inches long and 1 inch thick. Slice taffy into bite-size pieces, about 1 inch each.

7. Wrap each piece in a small square of parchment paper and twist ends to seal.

REASONABLY SIZED GUMMY BEARS

These gummy bears may not be the size of a small child, but they'll be just as tasty as the ones dotting the Chocolate Room. They're also a lot easier to eat. You can swap in honey for the corn syrup and fruit juice for the water to give these bears a grown-by-the-chocolate-river flavor.

MAKES 100 GUMMY BEARS

¾ cup cold water

6 (0.25-oz) packets unflavored gelatin

1 cup light corn syrup

1 cup granulated sugar

3 tablespoons sorbitol

2 teaspoons citric acid

½ teaspoon each 3 favorite candy flavorings

2 drops each 3 colors gel food coloring

Nonstick cooking spray

1. Add water to a large bowl and gently stir in gelatin until submerged. Let bloom for 5 minutes.

2. Add corn syrup, sugar, and sorbitol to a medium saucepan over medium-high heat and bring to a simmer, stirring continuously. Then reduce heat to medium and continue stirring, brushing sugar crystals from sides of pan using a wet pastry brush, until sugar dissolves and mixture is well combined.

3. Remove mixture from heat and stir in gelatin until melted. Then stir in citric acid until combined. Let mixture sit for 5 minutes. Use a spoon to remove any foam as it rises to top.

4. Strain liquid equally into 3 bowls. Stir ½ teaspoon of flavoring and 2 drops of food coloring into each bowl.

5. Spray a dry pastry brush with nonstick cooking spray, then wipe gummy-bear molds to lightly grease them. Use a candy dropper or carefully spoon mixture into molds.

6. Carefully transfer molds to refrigerator and let gummy bears set for at least 6 hours or overnight before removing from molds.

EXPLODING CINNAMON CANDY

Exploding candy for your enemies is all fun and games until it earns you a trip to the dentist. This cinnamon candy, on the other hand, is exploding with flavor but won't knock your teeth out, so you can enjoy it yourself and serve it to brave guests guilt-free. And you can work out your frustration with your enemies when breaking it.

························ **MAKES 2 POUNDS** ························

Unsalted butter, for greasing
1 cup water
3¾ cups granulated sugar
1¼ cups light corn syrup

1 teaspoon red liquid food coloring
1 teaspoon cinnamon oil
⅓ cup confectioners' sugar

1. Line a 15 × 10-inch jelly roll pan with nonstick aluminum foil and grease foil with butter.

2. Combine water, granulated sugar, corn syrup, and food coloring in a large, heavy saucepan over medium heat. Bring mixture to a boil, stirring occasionally. Cover and cook for 3 minutes, until sugar dissolves.

3. Uncover, increase heat to medium-high, and insert a candy thermometer into mixture. Let cook undisturbed until thermometer reads 300°F, about 25 minutes.

4. Remove candy from the heat and, keeping your face away from the pot, stir in cinnamon oil. Immediately pour into prepared pan and let cool completely, about 45 minutes.

5. Use the edge of a mallet to break candy into pieces. Sprinkle confectioners' sugar over entire surface of candy before serving or storing in an airtight container.

Dream Big!

Add a dash of cinnamon whiskey to the mix just before boiling for an extra jolt of flavor. (Don't worry, the liquor will burn off.)

RED CARPET FRUIT LEATHER

Few movie scenes are more iconic than Willy Wonka somersaulting on the red carpet to the delight of a concerned crowd. Gene Wilder himself came up with the stunt so that viewers would know they had to be on their toes. This chewy homage to his genius can be made with any fresh fruit, but strawberries give it that red-carpet color.

MAKES 10 PIECES

1 pound fresh strawberries

1 teaspoon lemon juice

1. Preheat oven to 170°F. Line a baking sheet with parchment paper.

2. Hull and rinse strawberries, then add to a high-speed blender. Blend until smooth. Add lemon juice and blend again.

3. Spread fruit puree onto prepared baking sheet and transfer to oven. Dehydrate for 3 to 4 hours, until center is no longer sticky.

4. Remove fruit leather from oven and let cool completely on baking sheet. Then transfer fruit leather and parchment paper to a cutting board. Using a pizza cutter or sharp knife, cut fruit leather into 5 long strips, then cut strips in half to make 10 pieces total, cutting through parchment paper.

5. Roll each strip with its paper to prevent sticking.

SWEET VIOLET BUBBLEGUM

If Violet only knew she could make her own bubblegum at home, it might have saved her a lot of trouble. You can even make three different, complementary flavors of gum (like blueberry, strawberry, and vanilla) and roll them together to create your own "three-course meal."

MAKES 15 PIECES

⅓ cup gum base
3 tablespoons light corn syrup
1 teaspoon glycerin
½ teaspoon citric acid

5 drops blueberry or other candy flavoring
5 drops purple gel food coloring
¾ cup confectioners' sugar, divided

1. Add gum base, corn syrup, glycerin, citric acid, and flavoring to the top of a double boiler over medium-high heat. Cook, stirring occasionally, until mixture is gooey. Remove from heat and stir in food coloring.

2. Create a mound of confectioners' sugar on a clean work surface, reserving 1 tablespoon. Make a well in center of sugar, then pour hot gum mixture into it. Allow to cool slightly, 3 to 5 minutes, until you can comfortably work with it.

3. Dust fingers with confectioners' sugar and knead a bit of sugar into gum mixture until sticky. Repeat with remaining sugar, kneading for at least 15 minutes, until gum is smooth, stiff, and no longer sticky.

4. Using your hands, roll gum out into a long, thin rope. Slice gum into bite-size pieces.

5. Dust gum with reserved confectioners' sugar, wrap each piece in a small square of parchment paper, and twist ends to seal.

SALTED CARAMELS

Veruca's attitude is a great reminder to temper your desserts' sweetness with a little salt—but just a little. No dessert should be as salty as she is. These caramels offer the perfect balance in one soft and chewy package. But if you prefer your salted caramel flavor with a side of creamy frosting, check out the cupcakes on page 68.

MAKES 40 CARAMELS

½ cup unsalted butter,
plus more for greasing
½ cup heavy cream
3 tablespoons water

¼ cup light corn syrup
1 cup sugar
½ teaspoon coarse or flaky salt

1. Lightly grease a 9 × 5-inch loaf pan, line it with parchment paper, and lightly grease paper.

2. Cut butter into 8 equal pieces, then add it and heavy cream to a small, microwave-safe bowl. Microwave in 30-second increments, stirring after each, until cream is hot and butter is melted, 1 to 2 minutes total.

3. Add water and corn syrup to a medium saucepan. Carefully stir in sugar to moisten, avoiding sides of pan.

4. Bring to a boil over medium heat, then cover with a lid for 1 minute.

5. Remove lid and insert a candy thermometer into mixture. Continue cooking until mixture reaches a temperature of 320°F, 5 to 10 minutes.

6. Immediately begin incorporating butter mixture in small increments. Caramel will foam and expand. Repeat with the remaining cream and butter (adding a sixth of it at a time, then stirring).

7. Once butter mixture is incorporated, continue cooking until caramel reaches a temperature of 240°F, 5 to 10 minutes more.

8. Immediately pour finished caramel into prepared pan. Let cool for 20 to 30 minutes before sprinkling salt over top, then let caramel cool for at least 3½ hours more.

9. Use parchment paper to lift set caramel out of pan. Using a sharp knife, cut caramel into bite-size pieces. Wrap each piece in a small square of parchment paper and twist ends to seal.

COST-SAVING POTATO CANDY

This Depression-era favorite is a big step up from cabbage soup but still an economical treat for anyone with a sweet tooth whose budget could benefit from time in the Taffy Pulling Room. If you've got a little extra pocket money for chocolate, you can always dip the pinwheels when they're finished.

MAKES 30 PIECES

1 medium russet potato

6–7 cups confectioners' sugar, plus more for dusting

½ cup creamy peanut butter

1. Peel and cube potato. Add potatoes to a medium pot and cover with water. Bring to a boil over medium-high heat and cook until fork-tender, 15 to 20 minutes.

2. Drain potatoes of all water, pat dry with paper towels, transfer to a large mixing bowl, and mash well. Let potatoes cool completely.

3. Using an electric mixer on low speed, beat in 6 cups of the confectioners' sugar, 2 cups at a time, until fully incorporated, scraping down sides and bottom of bowl as needed. Mixture should form a stiff, moldable dough. If too sticky or soft, add more sugar.

4. Lay a large rectangle of wax paper on a flat work surface. Dust with confectioners' sugar.

5. Roll out dough on prepared paper to create a rectangle about ¼ inch thick. Spread peanut butter evenly across dough.

6. Roll dough up from long edge to long edge to create a swirl and wrap tightly with wax paper. Transfer to refrigerator and chill for 1 hour.

7. When chilled, remove paper and slice into ¼-inch slices. Enjoy candy immediately or store in an airtight container in refrigerator.

CLASSIC CANDY DOTS

A fixture of every childhood (and Charlie's neighborhood candy shop), old-fashioned candy dots are the melt-in-your-mouth treat kids can't get enough of. And they're extremely easy to make at home. All you need is white copy paper and a few food-grade squeeze bottles.

MAKES 20 SHEETS

2 cups confectioners' sugar
5 tablespoons warm water
2 teaspoons meringue powder

½ teaspoon pure vanilla extract
2 drops each 3 colors gel food coloring
5 sheets white copy paper

1. Add confectioners' sugar, water, meringue powder, and vanilla to a medium bowl and mix with an electric mixer on medium speed for 5 to 6 minutes. Icing should fall from beaters in ribbons.

2. Divide icing mixture into 3 small bowls and stir 1 color of food coloring into each.

3. Spoon each mixture into its own food-grade squeeze bottle.

4. Lay 1 piece of copy paper horizontally onto a flat work surface.

5. Working with 1 color at a time and starting at left margin of paper, gently squeeze mixture onto paper to create a column of ¼-inch dots. Create 3 more columns in that color about 2½ inches apart. Next to first color, create columns with second color. Next to those, create columns with third color. You should have 4 sections with 3 colored columns each. Repeat with remaining paper and candy mixture.

6. Let finished candies set at room temperature for at least 6 hours or overnight. When set, cut paper into 4 strips so each strip has 3 columns of multicolored candies. Peel and enjoy.

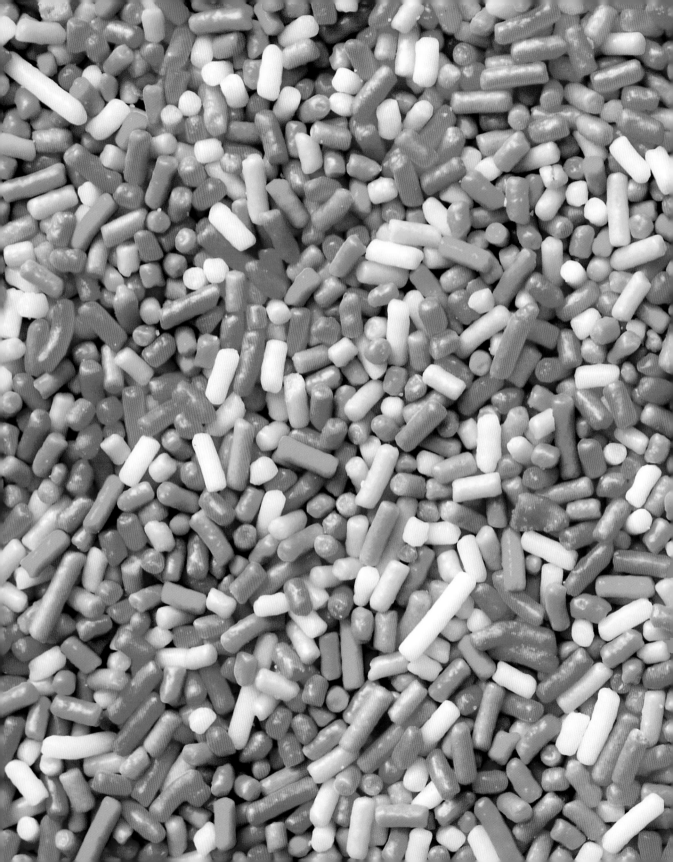

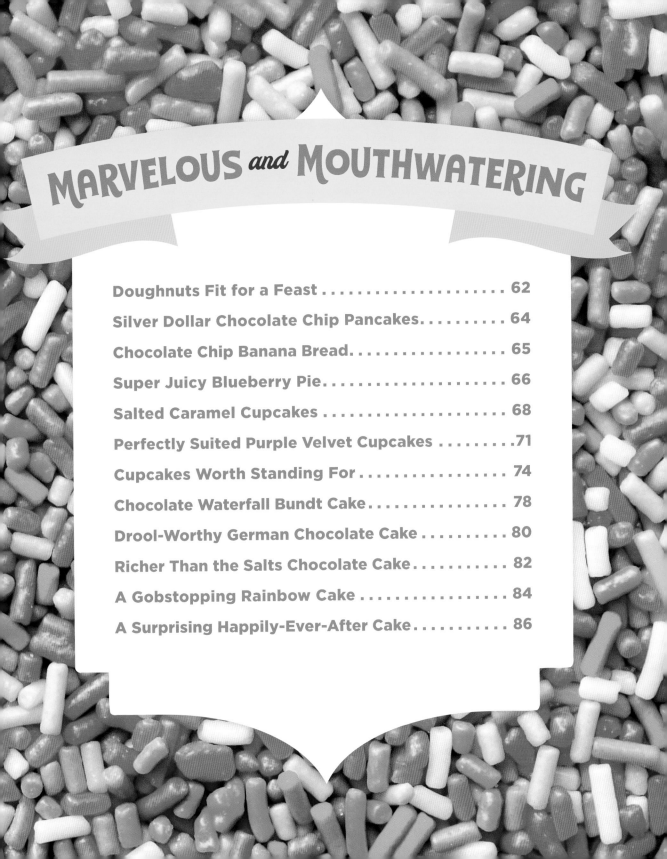

MARVELOUS and MOUTHWATERING

DOUGHNUTS FIT for a FEAST

Asking for a feast of doughnuts might be the most relatable thing Veruca does. These baked doughnuts are perfect for her imagined bean-feast (although that British tradition is typically reserved for employees—a title that Veruca will surely never hold).

MAKES 6 DOUGHNUTS

Nonstick cooking spray

For the Doughnuts

1 cup all-purpose flour

⅓ cup granulated sugar

1 teaspoon baking powder

½ teaspoon salt

1 large egg, at room temperature

⅓ cup plus 1½ tablespoons 2% milk, at room temperature

2 tablespoons unsalted butter, melted

1 teaspoon pure vanilla extract

For the Glaze

½ cup confectioners' sugar

½ teaspoon pure vanilla extract

Small pinch of salt

1–2 tablespoons 2% milk

2 drops pink gel food coloring

Sprinkles, for topping

1. Preheat oven to 350°F (176°C). Coat a 6-cavity doughnut pan with nonstick cooking spray.

2. To make doughnuts: Combine flour, granulated sugar, baking powder, and salt in a large bowl. In another large bowl, whisk together egg, milk, butter, and vanilla.

3. Add wet ingredients to dry ingredients and stir until well combined and free of lumps, being careful not to overmix.

4. Spoon batter into doughnut cavities, filling each three-fourths full. Transfer pan to oven and bake for 8 to 10 minutes.

5. Remove pan from oven and doughnuts from pan, transferring to a wire rack to cool completely. Meanwhile, make glaze: Whisk together confectioners' sugar, vanilla, and salt in a medium bowl. Then whisk in 1 tablespoon (15 milliliters) of the milk. If glaze is too thick, add more milk ½ teaspoon (2.5 milliliters) at a time. Whisk in food coloring.

6. Dip doughnuts into glaze to coat tops, twisting as you lift. Return to rack and top with sprinkles. Allow glaze to set at room temperature for 30 minutes before serving.

SILVER DOLLAR CHOCOLATE CHIP PANCAKES

Instead of using a found silver dollar to buy chocolate, skip the middleman and make silver dollars *with* chocolate. These pancakes whip up quickly and are equally delightful for breakfast or dessert. Whether you choose to top them off with chocolate syrup or maple is entirely up to you!

MAKES 12 PANCAKES

1 cup all-purpose flour
¼ cup sugar
1½ teaspoons baking powder
¼ teaspoon salt

5–6 tablespoons unsalted butter, divided
¾ cup 2% milk
1 teaspoon pure vanilla extract
½ cup mini chocolate chips

1. Combine flour, sugar, baking powder, and salt in a large bowl. Add 2 tablespoons of the butter to a small, microwave-safe bowl and microwave until melted, about 1 minute.

2. Whisk melted butter, milk, and vanilla into the dry ingredients until just combined. Use a spatula to gently fold chocolate chips into batter. Do not overmix.

3. Add 1 to 2 tablespoons of butter to a skillet over medium-low heat. When butter has melted, spoon 1 tablespoon batter into skillet. Repeat as space allows while leaving 1 inch between pancakes. Make sure butter reaches all edges of pancakes, using more if necessary.

4. When edges begin to brown, quickly flip pancakes and add 1 tablespoon butter to skillet. Cook until bottom has browned lightly, 1 to 2 minutes.

Chocolate Chip Banana Bread

The beautiful loaf of bread Charlie buys with his first pay does look filling, but Grandpa Joe is right—a banquet it is not. This chocolatey banana bread, however, is a meal unto itself. If you've never made banana bread with chocolate chips, you're in for a treat. They work as well together as the two Buckets themselves.

MAKES 10 SERVINGS

Nonstick cooking spray
2 cups all-purpose flour
1 teaspoon baking powder
1 teaspoon baking soda
1 teaspoon salt
½ cup unsalted butter, at room temperature
½ cup granulated sugar

½ cup packed light brown sugar
2 large eggs, at room temperature
1 teaspoon pure vanilla extract
3 large ripe bananas, mashed
1 tablespoon 2% milk
1 teaspoon ground cinnamon
1 cup semisweet chocolate chips

1. Preheat oven to 325°F. Coat a light-colored or glass 9 × 5-inch loaf pan with nonstick cooking spray.

2. In a large bowl, combine flour, baking powder, baking soda, and salt. In another large bowl with an electric mixer on medium-high speed, cream butter and granulated sugar and brown sugar. Beat in eggs 1 at a time until well incorporated, then beat in vanilla, scraping down sides and bottom of bowl as needed.

3. Stir in bananas, milk, and cinnamon, then add dry ingredients to bowl and mix on low speed until just combined.

4. Gently fold in chocolate chips, then pour batter into prepared loaf pan.

5. Bake for 1 hour and 10 minutes or until internal temperature of bread is 205°F to 210°F. Let bread cool in pan for 10 minutes before removing and transferring to a wire rack to cool completely.

SUPER JUICY BLUEBERRY PIE

Skip the three-course gum and go straight to the best part: the pie. This Super Juicy Blueberry Pie is bursting with flavor. And as long as you're careful not to drop any on your shirt, you won't have to worry about anything turning blue. If you notice the crust browning too quickly, cover it with aluminum foil when you decrease the oven temperature.

MAKES 8 TO 10 SERVINGS

6 cups fresh blueberries
⅔ cup sugar
¼ cup all-purpose flour
2 tablespoons cornstarch
¼ teaspoon ground cinnamon
2 tablespoons lemon juice

1 teaspoon lemon zest
2 store-bought roll-out pie crusts
or 1 recipe Buttery Pie Crust
(opposite), chilled
1 tablespoon cold unsalted butter, cubed
1 large egg beaten with
1 tablespoon water

1. Move oven rack to lowest position and preheat oven to 425°F. Line a baking sheet with parchment paper.

2. Add blueberries, sugar, flour, cornstarch, cinnamon, lemon juice, and lemon zest to a large bowl and mix to moisten.

3. Take 1 disk pie-crust dough out of refrigerator. On a floured work surface, roll out dough to create a circle 12 inches in diameter. Gently transfer dough to a deep 9-inch pie plate and press into dish.

4. Pour filling into pie dish, spreading evenly. Scatter cubes of butter evenly across top of filling.

5. Remove other disk of pie-crust dough from refrigerator and roll it into a 12-inch circle. Cut dough into long, 1½-inch strips of dough using a pastry wheel or sharp knife. Create lattice top by carefully weaving strips over and under one another. Press edges of strips into bottom pie crust edges to seal, then trim off excess dough. Crimp edges with fingers or a fork.

6. Lightly brush top of crust with egg wash.

7. Place pie on prepared baking sheet and transfer to oven. Bake for 25 minutes before reducing oven temperature to 375°F. Continue baking until juices are bubbling and internal temperature reaches 200°F, 40 to 50 minutes more.

8. Transfer pie to a wire rack to cool and set for at least 4 hours before slicing and serving.

BUTTERY PIE CRUST

Perfect for pretty much any fruit pie, this flaky crust comes together quickly. Make sure it has time to chill before you need it. And roll the dough gently from the center of the disk, turning it as you go, to keep it light and airy.

MAKES 2 CRUSTS

2½ cups all-purpose flour, plus more for rolling

2 teaspoons sugar

1 teaspoon salt

1 cup unsalted butter, chilled and cubed

½ cup ice-cold water, plus more as needed

1. In a large bowl, combine flour, sugar, and salt. Add cubed butter to bowl. Using a pastry cutter or 2 forks, cut butter into dry ingredients until pea-size and flour-coated.

2. Drizzle cold water into bowl 2 tablespoons at a time, stirring after each addition, until dough begins to feel moist and form large clumps. Use only as much water as is necessary.

3. Transfer pie dough to a lightly floured work surface. Using floured hands, knead dough until the flour is fully incorporated. Form dough into a ball and divide in half. Press each half into a 1-inch-thick disk.

4. Wrap each disk tightly in plastic wrap and refrigerate for at least 2 hours and up to 5 days.

Salted Caramel Cupcakes

For a dessert to be worthy of Wonka, it must have as many flavorful layers as the man himself. And this salted caramel treat takes the cupcake. Rich, savory, sweet, creamy, and hiding a caramel center, it's everything a dessert should be. You can top it off with your favorite frosting, but the White Chocolate Buttercream Frosting on page 77 is just sweet enough to let the caramel shine.

MAKES 20 CUPCAKES

2½ cups flour

2½ teaspoons baking powder

¼ teaspoon salt

½ cup unsalted butter,
at room temperature

1¾ cups sugar

2 large eggs, at room temperature

2½ teaspoons pure vanilla extract

1¼ cups whole milk, at room temperature

Salted Caramel Sauce (page 70)

White Chocolate Buttercream
Frosting (page 77)

1. Preheat oven to 350°F. Line 2 (12-cavity) cupcake pans with 20 liners.

2. Whisk together flour, baking powder, and salt in a medium bowl.

3. In a large bowl with an electric mixer fitted with a paddle attachment, cream butter and sugar on high speed until fluffy, 2 to 3 minutes.

4. Mix in eggs 1 at a time on medium-high speed until fully incorporated, then mix in vanilla.

5. Reduce mixer to low speed and mix in one-third of dry ingredients followed by half of milk just until incorporated, scraping down sides and bottom of bowl as necessary. Repeat once more, then finish with remaining dry ingredients. Be careful not to overmix.

6. Fill each cupcake liner to three-fourths full. Bake cupcakes for 18 to 20 minutes or until internal temperature reaches between 205°F and 210°F. Let cool in pan for 5 minutes before transferring cupcakes to wire rack to cool completely.

7. Once cupcakes are cool, use an apple corer inserted halfway into each cupcake to remove centers. Spoon caramel sauce into center, filling almost to top. Finish with a swirl of frosting.

SALTED CARAMEL SAUCE

Forget chocolate waterfalls—once you taste this rich caramel sauce, you'll want it flowing over every one of your desserts. The trick is to keep the sugar moving once it's in the pot. Swirl and whisk it until it comes together, silky smooth.

MAKES 1½ CUPS

1 cup sugar

6 tablespoons unsalted butter, cubed

½ cup heavy cream

1 teaspoon pure vanilla extract

1 teaspoon flaky salt

1. Sprinkle 1 tablespoon sugar into bottom of a heavy-bottomed 3-quart saucepan over medium-high heat.

2. Lift pan just above heat and swirl sugar until melted. Repeat with remaining sugar, sprinkling in ¼ cup at a time and swirling above heat until incorporated. When sugar is completely incorporated, it should be a dark amber color.

3. Whisk in butter until totally melted and combined. Remove pan from heat and slowly add cream, whisking rapidly until smooth. Then whisk in vanilla and salt.

4. Pour caramel into a heatproof container to cool before using or transferring to an airtight container to store in refrigerator for up to 1 month.

PERFECTLY SUITED PURPLE VELVET CUPCAKES

Not many people can pull off a purple velvet suit, but Gene Wilder as Willy Wonka
is certainly one of them. These purple velvet cupcakes celebrate that dashing
sense of style with a flavor just as memorable. Gel food coloring helps you get a
vivid purple batter, but you can use 2 teaspoons of liquid coloring instead.

MAKES 12 TO 15 CUPCAKES

1¼ cups all-purpose flour

½ teaspoon salt

1 cup sugar

½ cup unsalted butter,
at room temperature

1 large egg, at room temperature

1 teaspoon pure vanilla extract

½ cup buttermilk

2 teaspoons unsweetened cocoa powder

1 teaspoon purple gel food coloring

¼ teaspoon baking soda

2 teaspoons apple cider vinegar

Cream Cheese Frosting (page 73)

1. Preheat oven to 350°F. Line 2 (12-cavity) cupcake pans with 15 liners.

2. Sift flour and salt into a medium bowl. In a large bowl with an electric mixer fitted with a paddle attachment, cream sugar and butter until light and fluffy, 3 to 5 minutes. Add egg and mix well, then mix in vanilla. Reduce mixer to low speed and mix in one-third of dry ingredients followed by half of buttermilk just until incorporated, scraping down sides and bottom of bowl as needed. Repeat once more, then finish with remaining dry ingredients.

3. Add cocoa powder to batter and mix well. Then stir in purple food coloring. Mix baking soda and cider vinegar in another small bowl, add mixture to batter, and stir until well combined.

4. Fill each cupcake liner two-thirds full. Bake for 12 to 14 minutes, or until internal temperature reaches between 205°F and 210°F. Let cool in pan for 5 minutes before transferring cupcakes to wire rack to cool completely.

5. Add frosting to a piping bag with a star tip and frost cooled cupcakes.

Dream Big!

Give your frosting the same deep-purple hue by mixing in a few drops of food coloring. Then top things off with gold sprinkles or a piece of bright candy.

CREAM CHEESE FROSTING

Sweet, smooth, and just a little tangy, cream cheese is the Willy Wonka to buttercream's dependable Charlie Bucket energy. It's tailor-made for carrot cakes, pumpkin muffins, and red (or purple) velvet creations, but it's a delicious addition to any dessert.

MAKES 3 CUPS

8 ounces cream cheese, at room temperature

½ cup unsalted butter, at room temperature

3–4 cups sifted confectioners' sugar

1 teaspoon pure vanilla extract

⅛ teaspoon salt

1. In a large bowl with an electric mixer fitted with a paddle or whisk attachment, beat cream cheese and butter on high speed until smooth and creamy.

2. On low speed, beat in confectioners' sugar, vanilla, and salt for 30 seconds. Then increase speed to high and beat for 2 minutes more. For thicker frosting, beat in more confectioners' sugar ¼ cup at a time until desired consistency is reached.

3. Use immediately or store in an airtight container in the refrigerator for up to 5 days.

CUPCAKES WORTH STANDING FOR

Lush white chocolate buttercream and white chocolate ganache? If Charlie had whipped up some of these creamy cupcakes, Grandpa Joe would have stood up and put away that nightgown a lot sooner. Make sure you spring for the good white chocolate and not white chocolate chips for the smoothest flavor and consistency.

MAKES 12 CUPCAKES

For the Cupcakes
1¼ cups cake flour
¾ teaspoon baking powder
⅛ teaspoon baking soda
¼ teaspoon salt
5 tablespoons unsalted butter, at room temperature
¾ cup sugar
2 large egg whites, at room temperature

2 teaspoons pure vanilla extract
½ cup buttermilk, at room temperature

For the Ganache
4 ounces good-quality white chocolate, finely chopped
2 tablespoons unsalted butter
3 tablespoons heavy cream
White Chocolate Buttercream Frosting (page 77)

1. Preheat oven to 350°F. Line a 12-cavity cupcake pan with paper or silicone liners.

2. To make cupcakes: Whisk together cake flour, baking powder, baking soda, and salt in a large bowl.

3. In another large bowl with an electric mixer fitted with a paddle attachment, cream butter and sugar on high speed until fluffy, 2 to 3 minutes.

4. Mix in egg whites 1 at a time on medium-high speed until fully incorporated, then mix in vanilla.

5. Reduce mixer to low speed and mix in one-third of dry ingredients followed by half of buttermilk just until incorporated, scraping down sides and bottom of bowl as necessary. Repeat once more, then finish with remaining dry ingredients. Be careful not to overmix batter, which will be thick.

6. Fill each cupcake liner to between two-thirds and three-fourths full. Bake for 16 to 18 minutes or until internal temperature reaches between 205°F and 210°F. Let cupcakes cool in pan for 10 minutes before transferring to wire rack to cool completely.

7. Meanwhile, make ganache: Add chopped white chocolate, butter, and heavy cream to a double boiler and melt, stirring occasionally. Remove ganache from heat and transfer to a small bowl. Let cool to room temperature.

(continued on page 76)

(continued from page 74)

8. Using an electric mixer on high speed, beat ganache until pale and fluffy. Spoon finished ganache into a piping bag with the tip cut off.

9. Once the cupcakes are cool, use an apple corer inserted halfway into each cupcake to remove centers. Pipe white chocolate ganache into holes to top of cupcakes. Spread tops with a generous amount of frosting.

Dream Big!

Separate the frosting into multiple bowls, adding a few drops of gel food coloring to each to create deeply multicolored cupcake decoration.

WHITE CHOCOLATE BUTTERCREAM FROSTING

This heavenly take on buttercream frosting is like bursting through the roof of the Chocolate Factory and landing in the clouds. It's the perfect finish for white chocolate cupcakes, but it makes a dreamy topping for almost any dessert, from cakes to milkshakes.

MAKES 1½ CUPS

¾ cup unsalted butter, at room temperature

⅛ teaspoon salt

3 ounces good-quality white chocolate, melted and cooled slightly

½ teaspoon pure vanilla extract

1½ cups confectioners' sugar

1. In a large bowl with an electric mixer, cream butter and salt on high speed for 5 to 10 minutes until butter has doubled in size.

2. Mix in melted white chocolate on medium speed to combine, then mix in vanilla.

3. Sift in ½ cup of the confectioners' sugar. Mix on low speed, then medium speed, until fully combined, scraping down sides and bottom of bowl as necessary. Repeat with remaining sugar, ½ cup at a time. When last of sugar is incorporated, mix on high speed until frosting is light and fluffy, about 1 minute.

4. Transfer finished frosting to a piping bag fitted with a star tip for decorating cupcakes and other desserts.

CHOCOLATE WATERFALL BUNDT CAKE

The waterfall of chocolate sauce on this cake can't power a chocolate factory, but it is the only way to make this cake taste *just* right—which is to say, good enough to eat it by the handful. The secret ingredient is coffee, which deepens the chocolate flavor without leaving any coffee flavor behind.

MAKES 10 TO 12 SERVINGS

Nonstick cooking spray

For the Cake

2 cups all-purpose flour

2 cups sugar

1 cup unsweetened cocoa powder

2 teaspoons baking soda

1 teaspoon baking powder

1 teaspoon salt

2 large eggs

1 cup warm coffee or water

⅔ cup buttermilk

⅓ cup sour cream

⅓ cup vegetable oil

2 teaspoons pure vanilla extract

For the Glaze

6 ounces semisweet chocolate, roughly chopped

⅔ cup heavy cream

1 tablespoon corn syrup

1. Preheat oven to 350°F. Grease and lightly flour a 10- to 12-cup Bundt pan.

2. To make cake: In a large bowl, mix flour, sugar, cocoa powder, baking soda, baking powder, and salt.

3. Add eggs, coffee, buttermilk, sour cream, oil, and vanilla and mix using an electric mixer on medium speed until smooth, about 2 minutes.

4. Pour batter into prepared Bundt pan. Tap pan on countertop to remove air bubbles.

5. Bake for 45 to 50 minutes until cake reaches an internal temperature of 200°F to 210°F.

6. Transfer pan to a wire rack to cool for 15 minutes before turning out cake onto rack. Allow cake to cool completely.

7. To make glaze: Add chocolate to a large, heatproof bowl. Add cream to a small saucepan over medium heat and bring to a simmer. Then remove from heat and pour over chocolate. Let stand for 5 minutes, then stir until smooth and incorporate corn syrup. Drizzle generously over cooled cake and serve.

DROOL-WORTHY GERMAN CHOCOLATE CAKE

Just like the movie's setting, this classic cake's country of origin can be a source of confusion. The scrumptious chocolate dessert is actually American, while Charlie's seemingly English hometown is German (as were several of the movie's actors). The rich chocolate flavor created by the coffee beautifully balances out the sweetness of the coconut and buttercream frosting.

MAKES 10 TO 12 SERVINGS

Nonstick cooking spray

For the Cake

1¾ cups all-purpose flour

¾ cup unsweetened cocoa powder

1¾ cups granulated sugar

2 teaspoons baking soda

1 teaspoon baking powder

1 teaspoon salt

2 teaspoons espresso powder

½ cup canola or vegetable oil

2 large eggs, at room temperature

¾ cup full-fat sour cream, at room temperature

½ cup buttermilk, at room temperature

2 teaspoons pure vanilla extract

½ cup hot coffee or water

For the Filling

½ cup unsalted butter

1 cup packed light brown sugar

3 large egg yolks

1 (8-oz) can evaporated milk

1 teaspoon pure vanilla extract

2 cups sweetened shredded coconut

1 cup chopped toasted pecans

Chocolate Buttercream Frosting (page 35)

1. Preheat oven to 350°F. Coat 3 (9-inch) round cake pans with nonstick cooking spray, line with parchment paper rounds, then coat parchment paper.

2. To make cake: In a large bowl, whisk together flour, cocoa powder, granulated sugar, baking soda, baking powder, salt, and espresso powder.

3. In another large bowl with an electric mixer fitted with a whisk attachment, mix oil, eggs, sour cream, buttermilk, and vanilla until combined. Add wet ingredients to dry ingredients, then add the hot coffee and mix well.

4. Divide batter evenly among prepared pans. Bake for 21 to 25 minutes or until internal temperature of cake reaches 205°F to 210°F. Transfer cakes to wire racks to cool completely in pans.

5. Meanwhile, make filling: Add butter, brown sugar, egg yolks, and evaporated milk to a medium saucepan over medium heat. Stir and bring mixture to a low boil, whisking occasionally. Once boiling, whisk constantly until mixture thickens, about 5 minutes. Remove from heat and stir in vanilla, coconut, and pecans. Allow to cool completely.

6. To assemble cake: Use a large, serrated knife to even out tops of cake layers. Place a layer on a cake stand or serving plate and top with half of filling. Repeat with next layer and remaining filling. Top with the third cake layer and a generous amount of frosting, leaving sides bare. Transfer cake to refrigerator to chill for at least 45 minutes before slicing and serving.

RICHER THAN THE SALTS CHOCOLATE CAKE

No collection of Wonka-worthy desserts would be complete without a devilishly chocolate cake. This one's rich, fudgy flavor can't be beat, even by the Salts' bank account. It's topped with a luscious, whipped chocolate ganache, but it goes beautifully with any frosting.

MAKES 12 SERVINGS

For the Ganache
15 ounces semisweet chocolate, finely chopped
1½ cups heavy cream

For the Cake
¾ cup unsalted butter, at room temperature, plus more for greasing
2 cups all-purpose unbleached flour
1½ teaspoons baking soda
¾ teaspoon baking powder
¾ teaspoon salt
2 cups plus 2 tablespoons sugar
¾ cup unsweetened cocoa powder
2 teaspoons pure vanilla extract
3 large eggs, at room temperature
1¼ cups coffee or water
¼ cup whole milk

1. To make ganache: Add chocolate to a large, heatproof bowl. Add cream to a small saucepan over medium heat and bring to a low boil. Then remove from heat and pour over chocolate. Let stand for 5 minutes before whisking until smooth. Cover surface of ganache with plastic wrap. Let frosting come to room temperature, about 2 hours.

2. To make cake: Move rack to middle of oven and preheat to 350°F. Lightly butter 2 (9-inch) round cake pans and line bottoms with circles of parchment paper.

3. In a medium bowl, whisk together flour, baking soda, baking powder, and salt.

4. In a large bowl with an electric mixer fitted with the paddle attachment, beat butter at medium speed until smooth, about 2 minutes. Increase speed to medium-high and slowly add sugar, continuing to beat until light and smooth, about 4 minutes, scraping down sides and bottom of bowl as needed. Add cocoa powder and vanilla and beat on medium speed for 1 minute more. Add eggs 1 at a time until fully incorporated, beating for 1 minute between each addition.

5. Add coffee and milk to a small saucepan over medium-high heat and bring just to a boil. Remove from heat.

6. With mixer on low, beat dry ingredients into wet ingredients ¼ cup at a time. Carefully pour hot coffee mixture into batter and use a spatula to fold until well combined.

7. Divide batter evenly between prepared pans. Lightly tap each pan on counter to remove air bubbles.

8. Set pans on middle rack in the oven. Bake for 30 to 35 minutes, until cakes begin to pull away from sides of pans and center springs back when touched.

9. Transfer pans to a wire rack to cool for 10 minutes before turning cakes out of pans to cool completely on rack.

10. To assemble cake: Place a cake layer upside down on a cake stand or serving platter. Spread one-third of ganache evenly over top. Add remaining layer, right-side up. Cover top and sides with remaining ganache.

Dream Big!

Take this cake over the top with a drizzle of Salted Caramel Sauce (page 70) and a crumble of your favorite candy bars.

A Gobstopping Rainbow Cake

As delightfully sneaky and surprising as Mr. Slugworth (aka Mr. Wilkinson) himself, this plain-looking cake has a secret: rainbow-colored layers that are as fun as they are yummy. You'll create the rainbow colors by dividing the cake batter among six bowls and coloring each one a different rainbow shade, but the exact hues are up to you!

MAKES 14 SERVINGS

Nonstick cooking spray

¾ cup vegetable oil

2¼ cups buttermilk, at room temperature, divided

1 tablespoon pure vanilla extract

10 large egg whites, at room temperature

5¼ cups cake flour

3⅓ cups sugar

2 tablespoons baking powder

1 teaspoon baking soda

1 teaspoon salt

1½ cups unsalted butter, at room temperature

½ teaspoon each 6 colors bright gel food coloring

Vanilla Buttercream Frosting (page 35), quadrupled

1 drop purple gel food coloring

1. Preheat oven to 335°F. Coat 6 (8-inch) cake pans with nonstick cooking spray and line with rounds of parchment paper.

2. In a small bowl, combine oil and 1 cup of the buttermilk and set aside.

3. In a large bowl, whisk together remaining 1¼ cups buttermilk, egg whites, and vanilla.

4. In another large bowl with an electric mixer fitted with a paddle attachment, beat cake flour, sugar, baking powder, baking soda, and salt on low speed for 10 seconds to combine. Add butter to dry ingredients and mix on low until mixture resembles coarse sand, about 30 seconds. Then add prepared oil mixture and mix until moistened. Increase speed to medium and mix for 2 full minutes more, scraping down sides and bottom of bowl as needed.

5. Add egg mixture in 3 batches, mixing each for 15 seconds on low speed, scraping down bowl again.

6. Divide batter evenly among 6 bowls. Color each bowl with gel food coloring.

7. Pour each batter into a prepared cake pan. Bake for 20 to 24 minutes or until edges just start pulling away from pans. Remove finished cakes and tap pans firmly on countertop to release steam.

8. Let cakes cool in pans for 10 minutes before turning out onto wire racks to cool completely. (Can also freeze layers for 30 to 60 minutes before frosting to help layers set.)

9. In a large bowl, mix buttercream frosting with 1 drop purple food coloring to make frosting bright white. Assemble the cake in whatever order you like, frosting each layer with an even amount of frosting as you go. Use remaining frosting to frost top and sides of cake.

Dream Big!

Keeping this cake plain on the outside makes the inside all the more surprising, but you can decorate it any way you like. For a more colorful look, stir a couple more drops of food coloring into the frosting and top things off with your favorite candies.

A SURPRISING HAPPILY-EVER-AFTER CAKE

Covered with candy and hiding a sweet surprise inside, this cake is the over-the-top embodiment of Wonka's plot to find his successor. This recipe is all about doing what makes you happy, so fill and top it with your favorite treats. Keep things colorful by mixing 4 to 6 drops of your favorite gel food coloring into the frosting.

MAKES 14 TO 16 SERVINGS

Nonstick cooking spray

3¾ cups cake flour, plus more for dusting

¾ teaspoon baking powder

¾ teaspoon baking soda

1 teaspoon salt

1½ cups unsalted butter, at room temperature

2 cups sugar

3 large eggs, at room temperature

4 large egg yolks, at room temperature

1 tablespoon pure vanilla extract

1½ cups buttermilk, at room temperature

¾ cup rainbow sprinkles

1 tablespoon all-purpose flour

Vanilla Buttercream Frosting (page 35), doubled

2 cups assorted candies and sprinkles

1. Preheat oven to 350°F. Grease and lightly flour 4 (9-inch) cake pans, line with parchment paper rounds, then grease parchment paper.

2. In a large bowl, whisk together cake flour, baking powder, baking soda, and salt.

3. In another large bowl with an electric mixer fitted with a paddle attachment, cream butter and sugar on high speed for 5 minutes, scraping down sides and bottom of bowl as needed. Reduce to medium-high speed, and beat whole eggs 1 at a time until fully incorporated. Repeat with egg yolks. Beat in vanilla.

4. Reduce mixer to low speed and mix in one-third of dry ingredients followed by half of buttermilk just until incorporated. Repeat this once more, then finish with remaining dry ingredients. Be careful not to overmix batter.

5. In a small bowl, combine rainbow sprinkles with flour until coated. Gently fold into batter using a spatula just until incorporated.

6. Divide batter evenly among prepared pans. Bake for 25 minutes or until cakes reach an internal temperature of 205°F to 210°F. Transfer to a wire rack to cool completely before removing from pans.

7. To assemble cake: Using a 3½- to 4-inch round cookie cutter, cut a hole in center of 2 cake layers. Place a whole layer on a cake stand or serving plate and frost top of it. Top with a cut layer and frost top and inside of hole. Repeat with remaining cut layer. Fill entire hole with candies. Top with remaining whole layer and frost entire cake.

Dream Big!

Get the pictured look by using a lazy Susan and an icing smoother to smooth out the frosting, patting sprinkles around the bottom edge, and then chilling it and topping it with a drippy dyed white chocolate ganache (⅓ cup heavy cream plus 1 cup white chocolate chips, melted).

WHIPPED and WHIMSICAL

MULTICOLORED MARSHMALLOWS

Despite Mrs. Gloop's fear for Augustus's safety, Wonka's marshmallows surely don't contain children. Well, probably. But just to be sure, you can whip up these colorful treats yourself at home. And you can use them to decorate most other desserts, like the milkshake on page 120.

MAKES 117 MARSHMALLOWS

Nonstick cooking spray
1½ cups water, divided
3 (0.25-oz) gelatin packets
2 cups granulated sugar

¼ cup honey
1–2 drops each 3 colors gel food coloring
Confectioners' sugar, for dusting

1. Lightly spray a 13 × 9-inch cake pan with nonstick spray, line it with parchment paper, and spray parchment paper.

2. Add ½ cup of the water to a large bowl with an electric mixer fitted with a whisk attachment, and sprinkle gelatin on top. Set aside.

3. In a small medium saucepan over medium heat, combine remaining 1 cup water, granulated sugar, and honey. Insert a candy thermometer. Cook and stir until sugar dissolves, then let mixture continue to cook undisturbed until temperature reaches 240°F, 12 to 15 minutes. Remove from heat and pour mixture into a heatproof bowl to cool to 210°F.

4. Pour syrup mixture into gelatin mixture and beat on low speed until combined. Increase speed to high and beat until mixture triples in volume, about 10 minutes. Working quickly, divide mixture among 3 bowls and color each. Using a lightly oiled spatula, layer each color into prepared pan. Smooth surface and allow to set in a cool room for 8 hours or overnight.

5. When set, remove marshmallow from pan and peel parchment paper. Lightly dust top and bottom of marshmallow with confectioners' sugar. Lightly spray a serrated knife with nonstick cooking spray and slice marshmallows into 1-inch cubes. Cover cut sides with confectioners' sugar. Layer marshmallows between parchment paper in an airtight container and store at room temperature for up to 4 days.

COULDN'T-BE-EASIER CANDY CANE FUDGE

Candy canes, like Wonka's invitees, are more trouble than they're worth—when it comes to creating them at home, that is. This nod to Charlie and Grandpa Joe's choice treat from the Chocolate Room, however, is as easy to make as it is delicious. And vanilla fudge makes the perfect base for all kinds of candy—just make sure you swap out the peppermint extract for one that's complementary.

MAKES 64 PIECES

Nonstick cooking spray

2 (10-oz) packages vanilla baking chips

1 (14-oz) can sweetened condensed milk

1½ cups crushed peppermint candy canes

½ teaspoon peppermint extract

1 drop red gel food coloring

1. Line an 8-inch square baking pan with aluminum foil and spray with nonstick cooking spray.

2. Add baking chips and condensed milk to a saucepan over medium heat. Stir frequently until chips are almost melted. Then remove pan from heat and continue to stir until smooth and creamy. Stir in candy canes and extract.

3. Spread fudge evenly in prepared pan. Add food coloring and use a knife or toothpick to swirl it though the fudge. Transfer fudge to refrigerator to chill for 2 hours before cutting it into 1-inch pieces.

TRIPLE CREAM CUPS

It's hard to catch all of the amazing treats in Bill's candy shop, but one stands out as sounding particularly tasty: the Triple Cream Cup. This homemade take uses three creamy ingredients to make a mouthwatering chocolate treat, but it goes a step beyond the Candy Man's creation: you can customize the cream by swapping the vanilla extract for other flavors.

MAKES 40 CANDIES

½ cup unsalted butter, at room temperature

½ cup cream cheese, at room temperature

4⅓ cups sifted confectioners' sugar

1–2 teaspoons pure vanilla extract

1 (10-oz) bag dark or milk chocolate melting wafers

Sprinkles, for topping

1. Line a baking sheet with parchment paper.

2. Combine butter and cream cheese in a large bowl and stir by hand until no lumps remain. Stir in confectioners' sugar 1 cup at a time until incorporated.

3. Stir in 1 teaspoon of the vanilla, taste, and add more as needed.

4. Roll 1 tablespoon of mixture into a ball and place on prepared baking sheet. Repeat with remaining mixture. Transfer to refrigerator to chill for at least 45 minutes or overnight.

5. When candies are well chilled, melt chocolate wafers in a double boiler. Line another baking sheet with parchment paper.

6. Remove a few candies from the refrigerator. One at a time, use a fork or slotted spoon to dip cold candies in chocolate, allowing excess to drain. Place on prepared baking sheet and top with sprinkles while wet. Repeat with remaining candies, working in batches so candies remain chilled.

7. When all candies are coated, move baking sheet to refrigerator and allow chocolate to set for 10 minutes. Store finished candies in an airtight container in refrigerator. Remove candies 30 minutes before serving.

WHIPPED CREAM TEN WAYS

With so many incredible ways to customize whipped cream, it's easy to imagine why Mr. Wonka would devote an entire room to its creation. This recipe offers ten varieties you can use to top off other desserts—or just eat with a spoon, if you're so inclined!

MAKES 2 CUPS

1 cup heavy whipping cream, chilled

3–4 tablespoons confectioners' sugar

½ teaspoon pure vanilla extract

1. Chill a large mixing bowl and whisk attachment of an electric mixer in freezer for 10 minutes.

2. Add cream, confectioners' sugar, and vanilla to chilled bowl. Using an electric mixer fitted with chilled whisk attachment, beat on medium-high speed, scraping down sides and bottom of bowl as needed, until thickened and soft peaks form, 3 to 5 minutes.

Dream Big!

Turn plain whipped cream into a flavorful topping by adding any of these ingredients to the finished product:

- **Coffee:** 1 teaspoon espresso powder
- **Cinnamon:** ½ teaspoon ground cinnamon
- **Salted caramel:** 2 tablespoons Salted Caramel Sauce (page 70)
- **Peppermint:** ¼ teaspoon peppermint extract
- **Lemon:** 2 teaspoons finely grated lemon zest
- **Peanut butter:** 2 tablespoons creamy peanut butter
- **Berry:** 2 tablespoons berry jam
- **Maple:** 1 tablespoon maple syrup plus ¼ teaspoon maple extract
- **Chocolate:** 2 to 3 tablespoons unsweetened cocoa powder, added with the cream

HEAVENLY MERINGUE KISSES

Another confection spotted in the candy shop, these colorful meringues are light as air and perfectly poppable. You can give them away by the handful like Bill, but they're so delightful that you'll probably want to keep them to yourself. Make sure you wipe your bowl and whisk with white vinegar to give your meringue the clean slate it needs to thrive.

MAKES 24 KISSES

3 large egg whites, at room temperature

¾ cup sugar

½ teaspoon pure vanilla extract

¼ teaspoon cream of tartar

Pinch of salt

3 colors gel food coloring

1. Preheat oven to 225°F. Line a baking sheet with parchment paper.

2. Place the heatproof bowl of a stand mixer over a double-boiler. Add egg whites and sugar, and whisk until sugar has melted (temperature should read 110°F on a candy thermometer).

3. Transfer bowl to stand mixer and attach whisk. Whip mixture on medium speed for 1 minute, then add vanilla, cream of tartar, and salt.

4. Increase speed to high and beat until mixture forms very stiff peaks.

5. Prepare a piping bag fitted with a star tip. Dip a skewer into first color of food coloring and paint streaks on inside of bag. Repeat with other colors.

6. Spoon meringue into piping bag. Pipe kisses onto prepared baking sheet.

7. Bake for 1 hour, then turn off oven but leave kisses in place. Let sit in oven until completely cold, at least 1 hour or overnight, before enjoying or storing in an airtight container at room temperature for up to 2 weeks.

Dream Big!

Turn these kisses into colorful pops by piping the meringue in a circular pattern and inserting a lollipop stick ½ inch into the meringue while still wet.

FRENCH-SPEAKING MACARONS

Macarons may not all be chocolate, but these colorful treats would feel right at home in the Chocolate Room—especially since Mr. Wonka slips into French to avoid answering questions. This recipe gives you the basics for the classic vanilla treat, but the possible color and flavor combinations are as never-ending as a Gobstopper.

MAKES 30 MACARONS

For the Macarons
1¾ cups confectioners' sugar
1 cup finely ground almond flour
1 teaspoon salt, divided
3 large egg whites, at room temperature

¼ cup granulated sugar
½ teaspoon pure vanilla extract
2 drops gel food coloring
Vanilla Buttercream Frosting (page 35)

1. Add confectioners' sugar, almond flour, and ½ teaspoon of the salt to bowl of a large food processor, and process on low speed until mixture is very fine. Then sift through a fine-mesh sieve into a large bowl.

2. In another large bowl, use an electric mixer on medium speed to whip egg whites and remaining ½ teaspoon salt until soft peaks form. Slowly beat in granulated sugar ¼ teaspoon at a time until fully incorporated and stiff peaks form, then beat in vanilla.

3. Using a spatula, gently fold in food coloring just until combined. Then fold in sifted confectioners' sugar mixture one-third at a time. Continue gently folding batter until stiff enough to make a ribbon figure eight.

4. Spoon macaron batter into a piping bag fitted with a round tip. Pipe a dot of batter in each corner of a rimmed baking sheet and line sheet with parchment paper, pressing it into dots to keep paper in place.

5. Pipe 1½-inch circles about 2 inches apart onto prepared baking sheet, then tap sheet on a flat surface several times to release bubbles. Let macarons sit at room temperature for up to 1 hour until dry to the touch.

6. Preheat oven to 300°F.

7. Bake macarons for 17 minutes, until well risen and not sticking to parchment paper, then transfer to a wire rack to cool completely.

8. Spoon buttercream into a second piping bag fitted with a round tip. Pipe buttercream on bottom of 1 macaron shell and top it with another, bottom-side down. Repeat with remaining shells and filling.

9. Move finished macarons to an airtight container to set for 24 hours before enjoying.

Dream Big!

To create a rainbow of these French confections, make multiple batches at once and use a different food coloring in each. You can even go crazy and do the same for the filling!

DREAMY CREAM PUFFS

Whipped cream is so important to Wonka's operations that it gets its very own room. And what is a cream puff if not a delicate vehicle for delicious whipped cream? Fill these up with any of the delectable options on page 94 (or even the Bavarian Cream Filling on page 104) and they'll leave you dreaming only the sweetest of dreams.

MAKES 28 PUFFS

½ cup water
½ cup whole milk
½ cup unsalted butter
1 teaspoon granulated sugar
¼ teaspoon salt

1 cup all-purpose flour
4 large eggs, at room temperature
Whipped Cream (page 94)
Confectioners' sugar, for dusting

1. Move a rack to the center of oven and preheat to 425°F. Line a rimmed baking sheet with parchment paper.

2. In a medium saucepan, combine water, milk, butter, granulated sugar, and salt. Bring mixture just to a boil over medium heat, then remove it from heat and use a spatula or wooden spoon to stir in flour until fully incorporated.

3. Transfer pan back to stove over medium heat and stir for 1½ to 2 minutes until dough comes together to form a smooth ball.

4. Transfer dough to a large bowl. Using an electric mixer on medium speed, beat it for 1 minute. Mix in eggs 1 at a time until fully incorporated. Continue mixing until dough is smooth and forms a thick ribbon when lifted, about 1 minute.

5. Transfer dough to a piping bag fitted with a ½-inch round tip. Pipe 28 mounds onto baking sheet 1 inch apart, each measuring about 1½ inches in diameter and ½ inch high.

6. Bake puffs for 10 minutes in center of oven, then reduce temperature to 325°F and bake until puffs are golden brown on top, 20 to 22 minutes more. Transfer puffs to a wire rack to cool completely.

7. Transfer whipped cream to a piping bag fitted with a large open star tip. Pipe cream into cooled puffs by pushing star tip in or slicing tops off. Dust finished puffs with confectioners' sugar before serving.

Bavarian Cream Doughnuts

Whether you're indulging in a sugary breakfast or just feeling a little peckish while waiting for Wonka's gates to open like Augustus, these airy cream-filled doughnuts can't be beat. Add a tablespoon of brandy with the eggs for full authenticity.

MAKES 12 DOUGHNUTS

4 cups all-purpose flour, plus more for rolling

¾ cup granulated sugar, divided

1½ tablespoons dry yeast

1 teaspoon kosher salt

1 cup whole milk

⅓ cup vegetable oil, plus more for frying

2 large eggs

1 teaspoon pure vanilla extract

½ cup confectioners' sugar

Bavarian Cream Filling (page 104)

1. Add flour, ¼ cup of the granulated sugar, yeast, and salt to bowl of a stand mixer and combine by hand. On low speed, mix in milk and oil followed by eggs and vanilla until dough begins to form, about 2 minutes. Increase speed to medium and mix for at least 8 minutes or until dough is smooth and silky.

2. Cover bowl with plastic wrap and let dough proof at room temperature for 1 to 2 hours until doubled or tripled in size.

3. Punch down dough and transfer to a clean, floured work surface. Sprinkle flour on dough and roll out to create a ¼-inch-thick rectangle. Use a 2-inch cookie cutter to cut out doughnuts, rerolling dough as needed.

4. Lay a large rectangle of parchment paper out on a flat surface. Transfer doughnuts to parchment paper, cover with a clean towel, and let dough rise until doubled in size again, at least 30 minutes.

5. When doughnuts are ready, add 2 inches of vegetable oil to a Dutch oven over medium-high heat. Insert a candy thermometer into the oil. Line a plate with paper towels. When temperature reaches 350°F, gently lay 2 or 3 doughnuts in oil. Fry in small batches until golden, about 2 minutes on each side.

6. Transfer fried doughnuts to paper towel–lined plate to cool until they can be handled comfortably.

7. In a shallow dish, combine remaining ½ cup granulated sugar and confectioners' sugar. Dip doughnuts in sugar mixture to coat.

8. Spoon cream filling into a piping bag fitted with a star tip. Using a sharp knife, poke a hole in side of doughnut and create a pocket. Pipe cream into doughnut until slightly overflowing. Enjoy doughnuts immediately.

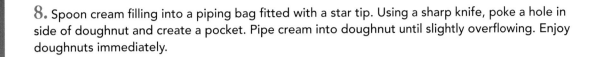

Dream Big!

There are no rules when it comes to fillings. You can swap out the Bavarian Cream Filling for jam, Vanilla or Chocolate Buttercream Frosting (page 35), Whipped Cream (page 94), Salted Caramel Sauce (page 70), or chocolate ganache (page 82) swirled with sprinkles.

BAVARIAN CREAM FILLING

Unlike single-minded Augustus, this custard cream is more versatile than it seems. You can use it to fill up pretty much anything made of fried dough (like doughnuts, cream puffs [page 101], and eclairs) or top it with fruit and eat it with a spoon like a rich, delicious pudding.

MAKES 1½ CUPS

1 cup sugar

¾ cup all-purpose flour

¾ teaspoon fine sea salt

3 cups whole milk

3 large egg yolks

2 tablespoons unsalted butter

2 teaspoons pure vanilla extract

½ cup whipping cream

1. In a medium saucepan over medium-high heat, whisk together sugar, flour, and salt with a whisk. Slowly whisk in milk.

2. Whisk egg yolks in a small bowl before whisking into mixture. Bring mixture to a boil, stirring constantly, until thick and pudding-like.

3. Remove pan from heat and stir in butter and vanilla until melted and well combined. Allow custard to cool completely. Meanwhile, in a medium bowl, whisk or beat whipping cream until soft peaks form.

4. When custard is cool, gently fold in whipped cream until combined.

WHOOPIE PIE MUSHROOMS

Delicate red velvet cake is enticing enough, but the real star of this show is
the fluffy marshmallow creme that fills out these Whoopie Pie Mushrooms.
No one would judge you if you were to eat it by the fistful like Mrs. Teevee.
Use a piping bag to pipe creamy dots of frosting onto each "mushroom."

MAKES 42 COOKIES

For the Cookies

2 cups all-purpose flour

2 tablespoons unsweetened
cocoa powder

½ teaspoon baking soda

¼ teaspoon salt

½ cup unsalted butter,
at room temperature

1 cup packed light brown sugar

1 large egg

1 teaspoon pure vanilla extract

½ cup buttermilk

2 tablespoons red liquid food coloring

For the Filling

4 tablespoons unsalted butter,
at room temperature

½ cup cream cheese,
at room temperature

1 (7-oz) jar marshmallow creme

1. Preheat oven to 375°F. Line 3 or 4 baking sheets with parchment paper.

2. To make cookies: In a medium bowl, combine flour, cocoa powder, baking soda, and salt.

3. In a large bowl with an electric mixer, beat butter on medium-high speed for 30 seconds. Beat in brown sugar until light and fluffy, then beat in egg and vanilla.

4. Reduce mixer to low speed and mix in one-third of dry ingredients followed by half of buttermilk just until incorporated. Repeat this once more, then finish with remaining dry ingredients. Be careful not to overmix. Use a spatula to gently fold in food coloring.

5. Spoon batter into 2-inch rounds (about ½ inch high) 1 inch apart on prepared baking sheets.

6. Bake for 9 to 11 minutes, until tops are set. Transfer baking sheet to a wire rack to cool completely.

7. To make filling: In a medium bowl using an electric mixer, beat butter and cream cheese on low speed until smooth. Fold in marshmallow creme. Sandwich a heavy dollop of filling between 2 cookies, then repeat with remaining cookies and filling.

KEY to the FACTORY LIME PIE

This pie may not be quite as sweet as receiving the keys to your very own chocolate factory, but it's pretty close. And making it is a lot easier than trying to survive Mr. Wonka's tour. Top it off with a dollop (or a layer) of Whipped Cream (page 94).

MAKES 8 SERVINGS

For the Graham Cracker Crust
5 ounces graham crackers
5 tablespoons unsalted butter, melted
⅓ cup sugar

For the Filling
3 large egg yolks
2 teaspoons lime zest
1 (14-oz) can sweetened condensed milk
⅔ cup freshly squeezed Key lime juice

1. Preheat oven to 350°F.

2. To make crust: Break up graham crackers, add pieces to a food processor, and process to create crumbs. Add melted butter and sugar, and pulse or stir until combined. Press mixture into bottom and sides of a 9-inch pie pan.

3. Bake for 8 minutes, until set and golden. Transfer pan to a wire rack to cool but leave oven on.

4. To make filling: In a large bowl with an electric mixer fitted with a whisk attachment, beat egg yolks and lime zest at high speed until very fluffy, about 5 minutes. Slowly add condensed milk and continue to beat until thick, 3 to 4 minutes more.

5. Reduce speed to low and slowly add lime juice, mixing until just combined. Be careful not to overmix.

6. Pour mixture into crust and bake for 10 minutes, or until filling has just set. Move pan to a wire rack to cool, then transfer to freezer for at least 20 minutes before serving.

SOUR LEMON TART

Charlie's tourmates might be sour about the snafus at the factory—assuming they make it out safely, like Mr. Wonka promises—but a little tartness can make the sweet stand out. This sunny lemon treat takes that lesson to heart with beautifully balanced flavors and textures. If it's a bit too tart, temper it with a topping of Whipped Cream (page 94).

MAKES 5 SERVINGS

Nonstick cooking spray

For the Crust
1 cup all-purpose flour

½ cup unsalted butter, melted

¼ cup confectioners' sugar, plus more for dusting

For the Filling
¼ cup granulated sugar

1 large egg

¼ cup whipping cream

⅓ cup freshly squeezed lemon juice

1. Preheat oven to 375°F. Generously coat an 8-inch round cake pan with nonstick cooking spray.

2. To make crust: In a large bowl with an electric mixer, mix flour, butter, and confectioners' sugar on high speed to form a soft, sticky dough, about 1 minute. Press dough into bottom and sides of prepared cake pan. Prick dough several times with a fork.

3. Blind bake crust for 20 minutes, until just golden at edges. Transfer pan to a wire rack to cool but leave oven on.

4. To make filling: In a medium bowl, whisk together granulated sugar, egg, cream, and lemon juice. Carefully pour filling into cooled pie crust.

5. Return pie to oven and bake for 35 to 40 minutes, until filling is set. Transfer pan back to wire rack to cool completely before removing tart from pan.

6. Dust cooled tart with confectioners' sugar and serve.

COOL and CREAMY

BUTTERSCOTCH RIPPLE ICE CREAM

Butterscotch ripple might only be 2 percent of invention according to Mr. Wonka, but it's at least 30 percent of this luscious ice cream. (With a flavor this rich, you wouldn't want more than that.) Alternating layers of ripple and ice cream ensures you get the perfect scoop every time.

MAKES 8 SERVINGS

For the Butterscotch Ripple
4 tablespoons unsalted butter
½ cup dark brown sugar
Pinch of kosher salt
2 ounces water
3 ounces heavy cream
¼ teaspoon pure vanilla extract

For the Ice Cream
2 large egg yolks
Pinch of kosher salt
⅓ cup plus 1 teaspoon granulated sugar
1 ounce water
10 ounces heavy cream
8 ounces sweetened condensed milk
2 teaspoons pure vanilla extract
3 ounces evaporated milk
3 ounces whole milk

1. Chill a 9 × 5-inch loaf pan in the freezer for at least 1 hour.

2. To make ripple: In a medium saucepan, combine butter, dark brown sugar, salt, and water over medium heat. Cover until butter melts.

3. Remove lid and cook over medium-high heat until butter browns and sugar caramelizes. Add heavy cream. (Mixture will bubble and expand.)

4. Remove pan from heat and whisk until butterscotch is smooth. Then return pan to medium heat and cook until butterscotch reaches a temperature of 240°F on a candy thermometer.

5. Pour into a heatproof container and stir in vanilla, then let cool to room temperature.

6. To make ice cream: In a large bowl with an electric mixer on high speed, beat egg yolks and salt until very light and creamy.

7. In a small saucepan over medium-high heat, combine granulated sugar and water and bring to a boil. Continue cooking undisturbed until temperature reaches 240°F.

8. While mixing on high, pour hot sugar syrup into yolks. Beat until very pale and thick.

9. In another large bowl with an electric mixer fitted with a whisk attachment, combine heavy cream, sweetened condensed milk, and vanilla on high speed until thickened.

10. Fold in yolk mixture, then continue whisking until very soft peaks form. Whisk in evaporated milk and whole milk until well combined.

11. In chilled loaf pan, layer in about one-third of ice cream. Transfer to freezer to chill for 45 minutes, then layer in one-third of butterscotch. Transfer back to freezer and chill for 45 minutes. Repeat with remaining ice cream and butterscotch, working with one-third at a time.

12. Cover surface of finished ice cream with plastic wrap and freeze for at least 8 hours or overnight before serving. Enjoy within 10 days.

Dream Big!

Chop up your favorite candy bar and layer the pieces in with the butterscotch ripple when freezing the ice cream.

BUBBLEGUM ICE CREAM

Need to break someone of a bad gum-chewing habit? This bubblegum ice cream gives you all the flavor with none of the chomping. It's also too tasty to last long enough to win any stomach-turning contests. (Sorry, Cornelia sweetie!) If you have an ice cream maker, churn as usual and add the sprinkles during the last 2 minutes.

MAKES 6 SERVINGS

2 cups heavy cream, very cold
1 cup whole milk, very cold
¾ cup sugar
2 teaspoons bubblegum flavoring

1 teaspoon pure vanilla extract
¼ teaspoon kosher salt
Pink gel food coloring
½ cup confetti sprinkles

1. Chill a 9 × 5-inch loaf pan in the freezer for at least 1 hour.

2. In a large bowl, combine heavy cream, whole milk, sugar, bubblegum flavoring, vanilla, and salt. Whisk for 2 to 3 minutes, until sugar dissolves. Add food coloring 1 drop at a time until desired color is reached.

3. Pour mixture into chilled pan and transfer to freezer to chill for 2 hours, stirring every 30 minutes. After final stir, top with sprinkles. Then freeze undisturbed for 2 more hours before covering surface of finished ice cream with plastic wrap. Freeze for at least 8 hours or overnight before serving.

Rainbow Drops Ice Cream

This bright take on simply delicious vanilla ice cream might not make you spit in different colors, but enjoying a dish of it is a good excuse to skip spinning through the darkness on that terrifying boat. And you're not limited to vanilla extract—swap in cotton candy flavoring to match the ice cream's pastel colors.

MAKES 6 SERVINGS

2 cups heavy whipping cream, very cold
1 (14-oz) can sweetened condensed milk, very cold

2 teaspoons pure vanilla extract
6 colors gel food coloring
Sprinkles

1. Chill a 9 × 5-inch loaf pan in the freezer for at least 1 hour.

2. In a large bowl with an electric mixer, beat whipping cream on high speed until stiff peaks form. In a medium bowl, combine condensed milk and vanilla until smooth. Gradually fold milk mixture into whipped cream.

3. Divide mixture among 6 small bowls. Add food coloring 1 drop at a time to each bowl to achieve desired colors, gently folding in each drop.

4. Drop ice cream mixture by the spoonful into prepared pan, alternating colors to create a mixture. Do not stir. Top with sprinkles, cover surface of ice cream with plastic wrap, and freeze overnight before serving.

BLACK RASPBERRY MADNESS ICE CREAM

If there's one takeaway from Wonka's factory, it's that candy making isn't all sunshine and rainbows. You need to balance the light with the dark. And for that, you can't beat black raspberry ice cream paired with semisweet chocolate. For the most intense flavor, use freshly picked blackberries.

MAKES 12 SERVINGS

2 pints fresh blackberries
1¼ cups sugar, divided
Juice of ½ lemon
1½ cups half-and-half

5 large egg yolks
1½ cups heavy cream
4 ounces semisweet chocolate, roughly chopped

1. Combine blackberries, ¼ cup of the sugar, and lemon juice in a large saucepan over low heat. Cook until blackberries are broken down and syrupy, about 20 minutes.

2. Pour mixture through a fine-mesh strainer into a large bowl. Use a spoon to push liquid through. Discard blackberry pulp and seeds and let mixture cool.

3. Meanwhile, combine half-and-half and remaining 1 cup sugar in a saucepan over medium heat.

4. In a small bowl, whisk egg yolks until pale and thick. Temper eggs by whisking a splash of warm half-and-half into yolks. Gently stir tempered yolks into saucepan. Reduce heat to medium-low and cook custard until thick, stirring constantly, about 5 minutes.

5. Pour heavy cream into bowl with berries, then stir in custard. Transfer mixture to refrigerator to cool for at least 30 minutes.

6. Freeze mixture according to ice cream maker's instructions or pour into a chilled 9 × 5-inch loaf pan and freeze for 4 hours. When frozen but slightly soft, stir in chocolate. Transfer to a freezer-safe container or cover surface of ice cream in loaf pan with plastic wrap. Freeze overnight before serving.

Peanut Butter Cookie Ice Cream Sandwiches

Finding a golden ticket may be important, but what would this scrumptious ice cream sandwich be without Mr. Salt's peanuts? It's a good thing he only loses five days' worth of peanut production to Veruca's search. This recipe uses vanilla ice cream, but you can use whatever flavor you like best paired with peanut butter.

MAKES 12 SANDWICHES

1⅓ cups all-purpose flour
¾ teaspoon baking soda
½ teaspoon baking powder
¼ teaspoon salt
½ cup unsalted butter, at room temperature
½ cup granulated sugar

½ cup packed light brown sugar
¾ cup creamy peanut butter
1 large egg
1½ teaspoons pure vanilla extract
3 cups vanilla ice cream
1 cup sprinkles

1. Preheat oven to 350°F. Line 2 (18 × 13-inch) baking sheets with parchment paper or silicone liners.

2. Whisk together flour, baking soda, baking powder, and salt in a medium bowl.

3. In a large bowl with an electric mixer fitted with the paddle attachment, cream together butter, granulated sugar, and brown sugar until combined. Beat in peanut butter, then beat in egg and vanilla. Mix on low speed while slowly adding in dry ingredients just until combined.

4. Drop 2-tablespoon rounds of dough 2 inches apart on prepared baking sheets. Lightly press each cookie twice with a fork going opposite directions to create a crisscross pattern.

5. Bake 1 sheet at a time for about 9 minutes, just until golden.

6. Let cookies cool on baking sheet for 5 minutes before transferring to a wire rack to cool completely.

7. Once cool, sandwich a generous scoop ice cream (about ¼ cup) between the bottoms of 2 cookies, using scoop to flatten ice cream to edges of cookies. Repeat with remaining cookies and ice cream. Press sides into sprinkles. Immediately wrap sandwiches in plastic wrap and freeze for at least 3 hours and up to 3 months.

HAPPINESS *in a* BERRY MILKSHAKE

This berry-vanilla creation is as over-the-top as Charlie's tourmates. But as Mrs. Salt says, it's happiness that matters most for a child. And this milkshake is sweet happiness in a glass. Top it off with whatever confections make you smile.

MAKES 1 SHAKE

4 ounces semisweet or dark chocolate, roughly chopped

2 cups vanilla bean ice cream

½ cup mixed berries

½ cup whole milk

Mini marshmallows or sprinkles

Whipped Cream (page 94), for serving

1. Chill a tall, freezer-safe glass in the freezer for at least 10 minutes. Meanwhile, microwave chocolate in a small microwave-safe bowl in 30-second increments, stirring after each, until melted and smooth. Set aside.

2. Add ice cream, berries, and milk to a blender and blend on medium speed until creamy and thick.

3. Pour marshmallows or sprinkles onto a shallow plate. Remove glass from freezer and dip rim in slightly cooled chocolate. Immediately press into candy to cover rim.

4. Pour milkshake into glass and top with whipped cream.

CANDY BAR MILKSHAKE

How do you go big on a milkshake? Decorating it with candy is a great start. But the Candy Man himself would flip (or somersault) for a milkshake *infused* with candy, like this one. This recipe uses a certain caramel-shortbread candy bar, but you can use any of your favorites.

MAKES 2 SHAKES

4 caramel-shortbread chocolate bars
3 cups vanilla ice cream
½ cup whole milk

1 tablespoon chocolate syrup, plus more for coating
2 tablespoons caramel syrup, plus more for coating
Whipped Cream (page 94), for serving

1. Cut 3 of the chocolate bars into small pieces. Split remaining bar in half and reserve.

2. In a blender, combine ice cream, milk, chocolate syrup, caramel syrup, and chopped candy. Blend on low, gradually increasing speed until milkshake is smooth.

3. Coat inside of 2 glasses with chocolate and caramel syrups, pour in milkshake, and top with whipped cream, drizzles of syrups, and candy bar half.

LICKABLE POPSICLES

All those fruit flavors seem wasted on wallpaper. But in a popsicle?
Now that's a perfect pairing. You can use whichever fruit tickles
your fancy, but berries are especially scrumptious.

MAKES 10 POPS

1 (13-oz) can full-fat coconut cream

3 cups fresh berries

¼ cup pure maple syrup

⅛ teaspoon cornstarch

1. Stir coconut cream in a medium bowl until well combined.

2. Add berries, maple syrup, and cornstarch to a blender and blend until smooth.

3. Spoon 1 tablespoon of blended berry mixture into bottom of each popsicle mold. Then spoon 1 tablespoon of coconut cream on top of berry layer. Repeat until molds are almost full, leaving ¼ inch of space at top for expansion during freezing.

4. Insert a wooden stick into middle of each pop and gently transfer molds to freezer to freeze for at least 6 hours or until fully frozen. Run molds under cool water for 5 seconds to unmold popsicles and enjoy.

GOBSTOPPER POPSICLES

Although the idea of a Gobstopper is great, that pointy confection would make for an awkward lozenge. These layered popsicles pack all that flavor into a much more enjoyable treat. Are they everlasting? No. Are they tasty? Absolutely.

MAKES 10 POPS

5 teaspoons each strawberry, orange, lemon, lime, blue raspberry, and grape gelatin powder

6 teaspoons superfine sugar
3¾ cups boiling water

1. Place each gelatin flavor in a separate small bowl. Whisk 1 teaspoon sugar into each bowl.

2. Working with 1 flavor at a time, pour ½ cup plus 2 tablespoons boiling water into strawberry bowl and stir gently until gelatin and sugar dissolve. Add 1 tablespoon strawberry gelatin to each popsicle mold. Freeze until just set, about 15 minutes. Repeat with remaining flavors in rainbow order.

3. When finished, place lid on mold and insert wooden sticks. Freeze until completely solid, at least 8 hours or overnight.

4. Run molds under cool water for 5 seconds to unmold popsicles and enjoy.

Mini Cherry Cheesecakes

Nothing goes better with a TV dinner than cherry cheesecake! These minis will feel like a feast to anyone who ends up on the wrong side of a miniaturization machine. Make sure your cream cheese is at room temperature before starting for the creamiest cheesecakes.

MAKES 18 CHEESECAKES

For the Crust
16 graham crackers
½ cup toasted pecans
¼ cup sugar
½ teaspoon ground cinnamon
4 tablespoons unsalted butter, melted

For the Cheesecake
2 cups cream cheese,
at room temperature
1 cup sugar
¼ teaspoon salt

⅓ cup sour cream
1 teaspoon pure vanilla extract
2 large eggs, at room temperature
2 large egg yolks, at room temperature

For the Topping
¼ cup water
1 tablespoon cornstarch
1 pound sweet cherries, pitted
3–6 tablespoons sugar
1 tablespoon lemon juice

1. Preheat oven to 350°F. Line 18 cavities of 2 cupcake pans with paper or silicone liners.

2. To make crust: In a food processor, pulse graham crackers, toasted pecans, sugar, and cinnamon until well mixed. Pour in melted butter while processing. Remove blades and use a spatula to fully incorporate butter.

3. Divide mixture evenly among cupcake liners, using a spoon to press crust into bottom of liner. Bake for 8 minutes, until fragrant and golden brown.

4. To make filling: In a large bowl with an electric mixer fitted with a whisk attachment, mix cream cheese on medium speed until smooth and creamy. Beat in sugar and salt until well blended, scraping down sides and bottom of bowl as needed.

5. Mix in sour cream and vanilla until combined, then beat in eggs and yolks 1 at a time until fully incorporated.

6. Spoon cheesecake mixture into prepared crusts, filling each liner about three-fourths full.

7. Bake for 18 to 20 minutes, then turn off oven and allow cheesecakes to rest inside for an additional 20 minutes.

8. Remove from oven and transfer to wire rack to cool to room temperature.

9. To make topping: Combine water and cornstarch in a small bowl.

10. Add cherries, 3 tablespoons sugar, lemon juice, and cornstarch slurry to a large pot over medium-high heat. Bring to a boil, stirring frequently.

11. As sauce thickens, taste and add more sugar if necessary. When sauce reaches desired consistency and taste, remove from heat and allow to cool completely.

12. Top each cheesecake with a couple of cherries and a spoonful of sauce. Enjoy warm or chilled.

Dream Big!

For the ultimate treat, freeze the cheesecakes and dip the tops into melted milk chocolate. Just melt 10 ounces of chocolate wafers in a double boiler, let cool slightly, and then dip the tops.

70% DARK CHOCOLATE PUDDING

Despite Charlie's teacher's comical shortcomings, using chocolate to learn about percentages isn't actually a bad idea—especially when it comes to bittersweet chocolate. Choose anything above 70 percent cacao for this recipe to make your pudding sing.

MAKES 8 SERVINGS

1 large egg

2 large egg yolks

6 ounces bittersweet chocolate

2 tablespoons unsalted butter, at room temperature

1 teaspoon pure vanilla extract

2½ cups whole milk

½ cup heavy cream

⅓ cup packed light or dark brown sugar

2 tablespoons unsweetened cocoa powder

2 tablespoons cornstarch

¼ teaspoon fine sea salt

Colored marshmallows, for serving

1. Whisk together egg and yolks in a small, heatproof bowl.

2. Add chocolate, butter, and vanilla to a food processor.

3. Whisk together milk, cream, brown sugar, cocoa powder, cornstarch, and salt in a medium saucepan over medium-high heat until smooth. Bring to a full boil, whisking, and let boil for 1 to 2 minutes more. When sauce thickens, immediately remove pan from heat.

4. Whisk a splash of hot mixture into eggs to temper them, then pour eggs into pan. Cook over low heat, whisking constantly, until mixture just begins to simmer. Immediately pour over ingredients in food processor. Blend until pudding is very smooth.

5. Divide pudding among 8 individual heatproof bowls or pour into a large serving bowl. Cover surface of pudding with plastic wrap (press against pudding to avoid skin forming) and refrigerate until firm and cold, at least 4 hours for individual servings or 8 hours for large bowl. Enjoy, topped with marshmallows, within 3 days.

FIZZY *and* LIFTING

GINGER ALE CITRUS PUNCH

This sunny citrus-rhubarb drink packs enough flavorful punch to power a train but is too delicious to use for anything other than drinking it. Slow down and savor it to avoid spilling it and you won't need the Wonkawash.

MAKES 12 CUPS

8 cups diced fresh or frozen rhubarb
5 cups water
1⅓ cups sugar
2 cups orange juice

¾ cup freshly squeezed lemon juice
4 cups ginger ale, chilled
Ice, for serving

1. Add rhubarb and water to a large saucepan over medium-high heat and bring to a simmer, cooking until rhubarb is soft, about 10 minutes. Remove from heat and allow to cool before straining through several layers of cheesecloth, discarding solids.

2. Measure out 4 cups juice and return to pan with sugar. Cook, stirring, over medium heat until sugar is dissolved, about 10 minutes. Remove from heat and allow juice to cool. (Can pour juice into a heatproof container and transfer to refrigerator for faster cooling.)

3. In a large pitcher, combine orange juice, lemon juice, and rhubarb juice. Refrigerate until cold. Just before enjoying, gently stir in ginger ale. Serve over ice.

CANDYMAKER'S DELIGHT

This sweet-and-sour drink is a fittingly surprising tribute to the renowned Candy Man. You'll infuse the limey lemonade with your favorite flavor (and color) of sour gummy candy. If you want to create multiple flavors, combine the juice mixture with the simple syrup and divide it among multiple containers before infusing each one with different gummies.

MAKES 6 TO 8 SERVINGS

7 cups water, divided
¾ cup sugar
3 large lemons
3 large limes

20 sour gummy candies
Ice, for serving
Lemon or lime slices, for garnish

1. In a large saucepan, combine 1 cup of the water and sugar and cook, stirring, over low heat for 5 minutes or until sugar dissolves to create simple syrup. Remove from heat, transfer to a heatproof container, and refrigerate for at least 30 minutes.

2. Meanwhile, halve and juice lemons and limes into a large bowl. Stir in remaining 6 cups water. Add gummies to bowl and allow to infuse for 20 to 30 minutes, stirring occasionally.

3. Strain lemonade into a large pitcher to remove gummy candies. (Discard candies.) Stir in 1 cup refrigerated simple syrup. Serve over ice, garnished with fruit slices.

PSYCHEDELIC SIZZLER

Like Mr. Wilkinson, this Gobstopper-inspired treat looks a lot more intimidating
(to make) than it is. Its rainbow layers are just a matter of chemistry, with the
denser liquids sinking and lighter liquids floating to create Wonka-like magic
in a glass. The result is a gorgeous fruity drink with a hint of fizz.

MAKES 8 SERVINGS

1 cup sugar

1 cup water

1 (0.14 oz) packet strawberry-
or cherry-flavored drink mix

1 drop blue liquid food coloring

2 cups club soda, chilled

4 cups orange juice, chilled

1. Combine sugar and water in a small saucepan over medium-high heat and bring to a boil. Boil,
stirring, for 3 minutes. Remove pan from heat and stir in flavored drink mix. Transfer mixture to a
heatproof container and refrigerate red syrup until cold, at least 1 hour.

2. Add food coloring to club soda and very gently swirl to incorporate.

3. To layer drinks, pour ½ cup orange juice into a snifter glass. Pour 2 tablespoons red syrup into
a spoon with its tip pressed against inside of glass so liquid travels down inside of glass to bottom.
It will settle beneath orange juice to create red layer. Slowly pour ¼ cup club soda into spoon
pressed against inside of glass to create green and blue layers on top of orange juice.

4. Serve immediately.

VIOLET LIME FIZZ

This violet-colored soda is as bubbly and tart as the talkative bubblegum lover herself but goes down much smoother thanks to the sweetness of fresh blackberries. It's also great for quenching your thirst when you've been over-juiced.

MAKES 8 SERVINGS

1 cup water
¾ cup sugar
1 pint fresh blackberries

1 large lime
8 cups seltzer water or club soda, chilled
Ice, for serving

1. Bring water, sugar, and blackberries to a simmer in a small saucepan over medium-high heat. Simmer until blackberries have broken down and mixture is syrupy, 15 to 20 minutes.

2. Strain mixture into a heatproof container, using a spoon to press berries to release all liquids. Discard solids.

3. Juice lime and stir juice into berry syrup. Cover and refrigerate until cold, 1 to 2 hours.

4. To make drinks, combine 2 to 4 tablespoons syrup with 1 cup cold seltzer water. Mix and serve over ice.

LIGHT-AS-AIR
Cotton Candy Mocktail

This fizzy drink might not make you fly like Charlie and Grandpa Joe, but its bright flavor will lift your spirits. And enjoying it doesn't require any lifesaving tricks. Just avoid dropping the cotton candy into the liquid or it will lift the fizz right out of your glass.

MAKES 6 SERVINGS

6 large lemons
1 cup sugar
1 liter club soda, chilled

4 teaspoons grenadine syrup
Cotton candy, for garnishing

1. Halve and juice lemons into a 2-quart pitcher. Stir in sugar and refrigerate for 30 to 60 minutes.

2. When ready to enjoy, chill glasses in refrigerator for at least 10 minutes. Add club soda to pitcher and stir in grenadine syrup.

3. Pour sparkling lemonade into chilled glasses and top with cotton candy, leaving a few inches between the treat and the liquid.

Dream Big!

Dip the rim of chilled glasses in melted dark or white chocolate, then in sprinkles, and top things off with a colorful or swirly straw.

DEW-SPRINKLED SUNRISE

When you need a sweet pick-me-up, this fruity soda will hit the spot.
Like the special mix Bill serves at the candy-shop counter, it tastes best
with a side of singing and, of course, plenty of confections.

MAKES 1 SERVING

Ice cubes

¾ cup citrus-flavored soda

2 tablespoons pineapple juice

2 tablespoons orange juice

1½ teaspoons grenadine syrup

1 orange slice, for garnishing

1. Fill a tall glass with ice. Add soda, pineapple juice, orange juice, and grenadine.

2. Stir and garnish with an orange slice.

SWEET-AS-NECTAR PEACH TEA

This peach tea is as sweet as the nectar of a teacup daffodil, but don't make the mistake of following Gene Wilder's lead and taking a bite of the cup. That daffodil was one of the few inedible items in the Chocolate Room—it was made of wax! Bite into some tea-soaked peaches instead for a far more satisfying experience.

MAKES 10 SERVINGS

For the Simple Syrup
1 cup sugar

1 cup water

2 ripe peaches, pitted and thinly sliced

For the Tea
8 cups water

3–4 tea bags

Ice, for serving

Peach slices, for serving

1. To make simple syrup: Combine sugar, water, and peaches in a small saucepan over medium-high heat and bring to a boil. Reduce heat to low and use a wooden spoon to stir and crush peaches into mixture.

2. Once sugar has dissolved, cover pan, remove from heat, and let steep for 25 to 30 minutes.

3. When simple syrup has finished steeping, strain into a bottle or an airtight container. (You can reserve peaches to use as a dessert topping.)

4. To brew tea: Boil water in a large kettle or pot, pour into a heatproof pitcher, add tea bags to taste, and steep for 4 to 5 minutes. Then remove tea bags and refrigerate tea to cool, 1 to 2 hours.

5. To serve, pour tea into glasses over ice and stir in simple syrup to taste. Garnish with peach slices.

CHOCOLATE RIVER COCOA

Not everything is better dark—the chocolate river in the tunnel of terror, for instance. But this rich, velvety, dark hot cocoa will soothe your frayed nerves and make that unsettling scene fade from memory. Use the highest quality chocolate you can find to make it Wonka worthy.

MAKES 4 SERVINGS

1½ cups whole milk
½ cup heavy cream
2 teaspoons confectioners' sugar
½ teaspoon espresso powder

8 ounces bittersweet chocolate, roughly chopped
Whipped Cream (page 94), for serving

1. In a medium saucepan over medium heat, whisk together milk, heavy cream, confectioners' sugar, and espresso powder. Bring just to a simmer, then remove from heat.

2. Stir in chopped chocolate until melted, returning pan to low heat if necessary. Serve warm, topped generously with whipped cream.

BUTTERSCOTCH BUTTERGIN HOT CHOCOLATE

It's no wonder Mr. Salt homed in on the "Butterscotch Buttergin" sign in the Inventing Room. A dash of butterscotch schnapps in comforting cocoa would certainly take the edge off for the adults on Wonka's tour. But if you prefer yours nonalcoholic, just swap in some butterscotch syrup for the schnapps and leave out the rum.

MAKES 1 SERVING

1 cup milk

1 tablespoon unsweetened cocoa powder

1 tablespoon sugar

Pinch of salt

2 tablespoons semisweet chocolate chips

⅛ teaspoon pure vanilla extract

1.5 ounces spiced rum

1.5 ounces butterscotch schnapps

Dash of orange bitters (optional)

Whipped Cream (page 94), for serving

1. Combine milk, cocoa powder, sugar, and salt in a small saucepan over medium-low heat and cook, whisking, until bubbles begin to form at edges of pan, 3 to 5 minutes. Whisk in chocolate chips until melted and well combined. Remove from heat and whisk in vanilla, rum, schnapps, and orange bitters (if using).

2. Pour finished hot chocolate into a large mug, top with whipped cream, and serve.

PURE IMAGINATION HOT CHOCOLATE

Who knew hot chocolate could be this beautiful? Also known as "unicorn hot chocolate," this Wonka-worthy beverage is an enchanting combination of flavor and nonsense. Garnish it with any of the treats in this book, from the Colorful Chaos Rainbow Bark (page 22) to the French-Speaking Macarons (page 98), for a truly over-the-top creation.

MAKES 2 SERVINGS

3 cups whole milk

2 tablespoons sugar

8 ounces white chocolate melting wafers

2 teaspoons pure vanilla extract

Red or pink gel food coloring

Whipped Cream (page 94), for serving

1. Add milk and sugar to a small saucepan over low heat and cook, whisking, until just beginning to simmer, 3 to 5 minutes. Whisk in white chocolate until melted and well combined.

2. Remove pan from heat and whisk in vanilla. Whisk in food coloring 1 drop at a time until desired color is reached.

3. Divide hot chocolate between 2 clear mugs and top generously with whipped cream.

Dream Big!

Dip the rim of your mugs in Vanilla or Chocolate Buttercream Frosting (page 35) or melted white chocolate, then in pink sprinkles. Finish things off with some Multicolored Marshmallows (page 90).

METRIC CONVERSIONS

If you're accustomed to using metric measurements, use these handy charts to convert the imperial measurements used in this book.

Weight (Dry Ingredients)

1 oz		30 g
4 oz	¼ lb	120 g
8 oz	½ lb	240 g
12 oz	¾ lb	360 g
16 oz	1 lb	480 g
32 oz	2 lb	960 g

Volume (Liquid Ingredients)

½ tsp.		2 ml
1 tsp.		5 ml
1 Tbsp.	½ fl oz	15 ml
2 Tbsp.	1 fl oz	30 ml
¼ cup	2 fl oz	60 ml
⅓ cup	3 fl oz	80 ml
½ cup	4 fl oz	120 ml
⅔ cup	5 fl oz	160 ml
¾ cup	6 fl oz	180 ml
1 cup	8 fl oz	240 ml
1 pt	16 fl oz	480 ml
1 qt	32 fl oz	960 ml

Oven Temperatures

Fahrenheit	Celsius	Gas Mark
225°	110°	¼
250°	120°	½
275°	140°	1
300°	150°	2
325°	160°	3
350°	180°	4
375°	190°	5
400°	200°	6
425°	220°	7
450°	230°	8

Length

¼ in	6 mm
½ in	13 mm
¾ in	19 mm
1 in	25 mm
6 in	15 cm
12 in	30 cm

INDEX